P9-CSU-744

JOURNAL FOR THE STUDY OF THE OLD TESTAMENT
SUPPLEMENT SERIES
222

Editors
David J.A. Clines
Philip R. Davies

Executive Editor
John Jarick

Editorial Board
Robert P. Carroll, Richard J. Coggins, Alan Cooper, J. Cheryl Exum,
John Goldingay, Robert P. Gordon, Norman K. Gottwald,
Andrew D.H. Mayes, Carol Meyers, Patrick D. Miller

Sheffield Academic Press

Reading the Psalms as a Book

Norman Whybray

Journal for the Study of the Old Testament
Supplement Series 222

Copyright © 1996 Sheffield Academic Press

Published by Sheffield Academic Press Ltd
Mansion House
19 Kingfield Road
Sheffield S11 9AS
England

Printed on acid-free paper in Great Britain
by Bookcraft Ltd
Midsomer Norton, Bath

British Library Cataloguing in Publication Data

A catalogue record for this book is available
from the British Library

ISBN 1-85075-622-8
1-85075-797-6 pbk

CONTENTS

Abbreviations 7
Note on Commentaries 9

INTRODUCTION 11

Chapter 1
RECENT VIEWS ON THE COMPOSITION AND ARRANGEMENT OF THE PSALTER 15

Chapter 2
WISDOM AND TORAH MATERIAL 36

Chapter 3
ESCHATOLOGICAL INTERPRETATION 88

Chapter 4
THE INTERPRETATION OF RITUAL SACRIFICE 100

CONCLUSION 118

Bibliography 125
Index of References 129
Index of Authors 136

ABBREVIATIONS

AB	Anchor Bible
AOAT	Alter Orient und Altes Testament
ATD	Das Alte Testament Deutsch
BASOR	*Bulletin of the American Schools of Oriental Research*
BETL	Bibliotheca ephemeridum theologicarum lovaniensium
BHS	*Biblia hebraica stuttgartensia*
BKAT	Biblischer Kommentar: Altes Testament
BZAW	Beihefte zur *ZAW*
HAT	Handbuch zum Alten Testament
HKAT	Handkommentar zum Alten Testament
ICC	International Critical Commentary
Int	*Interpretation*
JBL	*Journal of Biblical Literature*
JSOT	*Journal for the Study of the Old Testament*
JSOTSup	*Journal for the Study of the Old Testament*, Supplement Series
KHC	Kurzer Hand-Commentar zum Alten Testament
NCB	New Century Bible
OTL	Old Testament Library
OTS	*Oudtestamentische Studiën*
RB	*Revue biblique*
SBL	Society of Biblical Literature
SBLDS	Society of Biblical Literature Dissertation Series
SNVAO	Skrifter utgitt av det norske videnskaps-akademi i Oslo
TBAT	Theologische Bücherei, Altes Testament
TBC	Torch Bible Commentaries
TDOT	G.J. Botterweck and H. Ringgren (eds.), *Theological Dictionary of the Old Testament*
THAT	E. Jenni and C. Westermann (eds.), *Theologisches Handwörterbuch zum Alten Testament*
VT	*Vetus Testamentum*
VTSup	*Vetus Testamentum*, Supplements
WBC	Word Biblical Commentary
WC	Westminster Commentaries
ZAW	*Zeitschrift für die alttestamentliche Wissenschaft*

NOTE ON COMMENTARIES

The following commentaries are indicated only by the authors' surnames when the references are to particular psalms:

L.C. Allen, *Psalms 101–150* (WBC; Waco, TX: Word Books, 1983).

A.A. Anderson, *The Book of Psalms* (NCB; 2 vols.; London: Marshall, Morgan & Scott, 1972).

W.E. Barnes, *The Psalms with Introduction and Notes* (WC; 2 vols.; London: Methuen; Philadelphia: Westminster Press, 1931).

C.A. Briggs, *The Book of Psalms* (ICC; 2 vols.; Edinburgh: T. & T. Clark, 1906, 1907).

P.C. Craigie, *Psalms 1–50* (WBC; Waco, TX: Word Books, 1983).

M. Dahood, *Psalms* (AB; 3 vols.; Garden City, NY: Doubleday, 1966, 1968, 1970).

B. Duhm, *Die Psalmen* (KHC, 1899).

J.H. Eaton, *Psalms: Introduction and Commentary* (TBC, 1967).

H. Gunkel, *Die Psalmen übersetzt und erklärt* (HKAT; Göttingen: Vandenhoeck & Ruprecht, 1929).

L. Jacquet, *Les psaumes et le coeur de l'homme: Etude textuelle, littéraire et doctrinale* (3 vols.; Gembloux: Duculot, 1975, 1977, 1979).

H.-J. Kraus, *Psalmen* (BKAT; 2 vols.; Neukirchen–Vluyn: Neukirchener Verlag, 1961).

W.O.E. Oesterley, *The Psalms Translated with Text-Critical and Exegetical Notes* (2 vols.; London: SPCK, 1939).

H. Schmidt, *Die Psalmen* (HAT; Tübingen: Mohr, 1934).

M.E. Tate, *Psalms 51–100* (WBC; Waco, TX: Word Books, 1990).

A. Weiser, *Die Psalmen* (ATD; Göttingen: Vandenhoeck & Ruprecht, 5th edn, 1959); ET *The Psalms* (OTL; London: SCM Press, 1962).

INTRODUCTION

The Psalms have been used as a source of spiritual refreshment and private devotion, as well as part of public, collective worship, by both Jewish and Christian believers throughout the centuries from very early times to the present day. For many, they have been a treasury of faith to be drawn on in every situation in life, giving expression as they do to every mood of the believer from near despair to the serenity that finds its outlet in praise and thanksgiving.[1] They have also been taken by many as *models* of prayer: many modern hymns, for example, are paraphrases of psalms or have been based on psalmic themes. Such use of the Psalms has often been selective: particular psalms have been chosen as models because they have been thought to express particular articles of belief, or because they embody particular religious emotions.

One of the most significant ways in which the Psalter has been used and is still used today is the practice of reading or reciting it, for purposes of meditation, *consecutively*, from beginning to end. In doing this, readers find themselves caught up in worship not merely into moods that they find most congenial at the moment of reading, but successively into a variety of different moods, and in an order that they have not chosen for themselves but that has already been laid down for them. They are thus constrained to enter into the whole range of human situations, with which they can in some sense empathize and so adapt to their faith. The most striking example of this practice is the Holy Office devised by the early church in which the whole Psalter is recited, in order, every week[2] (or, in the Church of England, every month[3]) in daily

1. See R.E. Prothero, *The Psalms in Human Life* (London: Nelson/John Murray, 1903).

2. *The Rule of Saint Benedict*; *The Roman Breviary*. See L. Jacquet, *Les psaumes et le coeur de l'homme: Etude textuelle, littéraire et doctrinale* (Gembloux: Duculot), I, especially pp. 192-95 for the origin and history of this practice.

3. *The Book of Common Prayer and Administration of the Sacraments and Other Rites and Ceremonies of the Church According to the Use of the Church of England* under the rubric 'The Order How the Psalter is Appointed to be Read'.

prayer. Although these offices were designed for corporate prayer it is also intended that the participants should use the psalms for private meditation, suitable intervals being provided for reflection on the psalms' meaning for their own spiritual development.

Only recently have some scholars suggested that the use of the Psalter as a book of private devotion may have originated earlier than had previously been supposed: that it was contemporary with the final compilation of the Psalter itself, and therefore that its final shape and arrangement are not haphazard and random, as has generally been believed, but were contrived in order to make it a book that could be read consecutively by pious individuals as a basis for meditation, following a schema which could lead the readers to develop their spirituality in an ordered way.

That the composition of the Psalter was completed at a fairly late, certainly post-exilic date is generally accepted. But the opinion, associated especially with the names of Hermann Gunkel[4] and Sigmund Mowinckel,[5] that the great majority of the psalms were composed for *public*, cultic use, became almost axiomatic in Psalms scholarship and has remained so throughout the present century. At the same time, modern research also led to the identification of a relatively small number of psalms that appeared to be unconnected with Israel's public cult and to be of a private nature. Gunkel had already noted the existence in the Psalter of a group of psalms which he called *Weisheitsgedichte*, 'wisdom poems', which could not be fitted into any of the formal categories into which he had placed most of the other psalms.[6] These wisdom poems bore close similarities to the wisdom books of the Old Testament, but did not all originate in the same period: Gunkel saw them as representing different stages in the development of the concept of wisdom ranging from a rather secular pre-exilic wisdom to a later concern with the problem of retribution; but he proposed post-exilic dates for at least Psalms 1, 37, 73, 91, 112, 119 and 128. Among these he noted some which express a particular devotion to the Law of Moses, reflecting a kind of 'law piety' in which the Law had become the central

4. H. Gunkel, *Die Psalmen übersetzt und erklärt* (HKAT; Göttingen: Vandenhoeck & Ruprecht, 1929): *Einleitung in die Psalmen* (Göttingen: Vandenhoeck & Ruprecht, 1933).

5. S. Mowinckel, *Psalmenstudien* (6 vols.; Oslo, 1921–24); *The Psalms in Israel's Worship* (2 vols.; Oxford: Basil Blackwell, 1962 [translated with revisions from the Norwegian *Offersang og Sangoffer* (Oslo: Aschehoug, 1951)].

6. *Einleitung in die Psalmen*, pp. 381-97.

feature of Jewish belief. These he held to be the latest in date. It was his opinion that these wisdom psalms and Law psalms had never been connected with the public cult; and he accounted for their presence among what was primarily a collection of cultic poems by surmising that their inclusion was a consequence of demands to the priests by the laity.

Chapter 1

RECENT VIEWS ON THE COMPOSITION AND ARRANGEMENT OF THE PSALTER

The work of Gunkel on the Psalms set the course for psalms scholarship for many decades. Since then, however, one particular aspect of the Psalter has been plagued by problems to which no agreed solution has been found. The first of these is the definition and identification of wisdom psalms: no two scholars have agreed about which psalms belong to this category, and it has not even been possible to establish agreed criteria for their identification.[1] This is partly due to their diversity of form: unlike the psalms in Gunkel's other categories (laments, hymns of thanksgiving, hymns of praise and so on) they do not conform to any stylistic pattern or regular thematic sequence. Gunkel himself noted that some psalms which he designated wisdom psalms are couched in the forms of quite different categories, such as that of psalms of thanksgiving. The second problem is that of authorship—or, more accurately, of the identification of the social, professional or religious class or classes to which the authors of the wisdom psalms belonged. This problem is more acute here than in the case of the other psalms, whose cultic affinities are clearly apparent.

Sigmund Mowinckel, second only to Gunkel as a pioneer of modern psalms study, had already in 1924, some years before the publication of Gunkel's monumental study, drawn attention to the possibility of 'private psalmody'.[2] He returned to the subject in 1951[3] and 1955,[4] when he

1. This problem has been widely discussed. See most recently R.N. Whybray, 'Wisdom Psalms', in J. Day, R.P. Gordon and H.G.M. Williamson (eds.), *Wisdom in Ancient Israel: Essays in Honour of J.A. Emerton* (Cambridge: Cambridge University Press, 1995), pp. 152-60.

2. *Psalmenstudien*, VI, pp. 8-36.

3. *Offersang og Sangoffer* (see *The Psalms in Israel's Worship*, II, pp. 104-14).

4. 'Psalms and Wisdom', in M. Noth and D.W. Thomas (eds.), *Wisdom in*

offered a more precise explanation of the authorship of the wisdom psalms than Gunkel's rather vague suggestion of lay pressure on the temple priesthood. In his last contribution to the subject he postulated the existence of a school for scribes, who for him were identical with the 'wise men', closely connected with the Second Temple in Jerusalem. This school was thus in close touch with the temple singers who were responsible for the traditional psalms. It was the function of these learned scribes to preserve the Psalter for posterity. But some of them were also poets; and their poems were probably recited before the students in the scribal school. In this way there developed a 'learned psalmography' of a private nature, perhaps intended as a substitute for animal sacrifice. In addition to 'wisdom', praise of the Law was also a major theme of their psalms. In the course of time these more recently composed psalms came to be included in the 'official' collection, since their authors were themselves the collectors and redactors of the Psalter.

The view of Jansen was somewhat similar to that of Mowinckel.[5] He also maintained that these psalms were the work of scribes who taught in a school attached to the temple; but this institution was not restricted to the training of temple scribes. Under the monarchy it had been the training centre for court scribes as well, and subsequently for law scribes. Since the court scribes and their successors included the authors of wisdom books, and wisdom and religious texts were studied together, there was a mingling of literary traditions which led ultimately to the composition of wisdom psalms. Jansen admitted the scarcity of evidence to support his theory. He cited a handful of Old Testament texts, notably 1 Chron. 25.8, in which the terms *talmîd*, 'pupil', and *mēbîn*, 'teacher', occur, but relied mainly on analogies with Egyptian and Mesopotamian temple schools.

Mowinckel's and Jansen's attempts to identify so precisely the milieu and authorship of the wisdom psalms were extremely speculative, based on scanty evidence of questionable character. The notion of a temple school in Israel in Old Testament times, though supported as late as 1970 by von Rad,[6] has more recently been discarded, often together with the notion of Israelite schools in general, for lack of direct evidence; and

Israel and in the Ancient Near East, Presented to Professor Harold Henry Rowley (VTSup, 3; Leiden: Brill, 1955), pp. 205-24.

5. H.L. Jansen, *Die spätjüdische Psalmendichtung* (SNVAO, 3; Oslo, 1937).

6. G. von Rad, *Weisheit in Israel* (Neukirchen–Vluyn: Neukirchener Verlag, 1970), pp. 31-32 (ET *Wisdom in Israel* [London: SCM Press, 1972], pp. 17-18.)

the value of Egyptian and Mesopotamian models has been increasingly questioned.[7] However, the fact of the presence of apparently 'non-cultic' psalms in a Psalter consisting predominantly of compositions originally intended for cultic use remains a problem. But Mowinckel's suggestion that the authors of the 'learned psalmography' were themselves the final compilers of the Psalter has proved to be a fruitful one.

In 1963 Murphy made a notable attempt to examine the criteria for the classification of wisdom psalms and to discuss their life-setting.[8] With regard to criteria he largely followed Gunkel: he listed in particular the recurrence of characteristic motifs. But the criteria were to be used in a broad sense, since these psalms do not belong to a *Gattung* in the strict sense of that term. Murphy also named life-setting among his criteria, but in opposition to Mowinckel, Jansen and others he maintained that 'their demonstration has shown only that these poems are the product of the sages, that they spring from the *milieu sapiential*; it has not captured the precise life setting of the alleged wisdom psalms'.[9] Murphy also pointed to the elements of thanksgiving or testimony and of didactic purpose as characteristic of some of these psalms, and suggested that the view that they are non-cultic may not necessarily be correct: 'It is not apparent why the wisdom psalms should be excluded from the cult.'[10] He argued that the cult—that is, public worship—was more varied than has often been supposed, and in particular that the post-exilic cult was not identical with the pre-exilic: the element of testimony was more marked, and took on a more didactic character which linked wisdom to worship. Murphy named Psalms 1, 32, 34, 37, 49, 112 and 128 as wisdom psalms; but he remarked that there are many other psalms in the Psalter that contain wisdom elements. These show that 'the psalmists found wisdom themes useful and that they exploited the wisdom style as an apt mode of expression'.[11] He did not, however, consider another possibility: that in some cases such wisdom elements may have been

7. For instance by B. Lang, 'Schule und Unterricht im alten Israel', in M. Gilbert (ed.), *La Sagesse de l'Ancien Testament* (BETL, 51; Gembloux: Duculot; Leuven: Leuven University Press, 1979), pp. 186-201; F.W. Golka, 'Die israelitische Weisheitsschule oder "des Kaisers neue Kleider"', *VT* 33 (1983), pp. 257-71.

8. R.E. Murphy, 'A Consideration of the Classification "Wisdom Psalms"', in J.A. Emerton (ed.), *Congress Volume, Bonn, 1962* (VTSup, 9; Leiden: Brill, 1963), pp. 156-67.

9. 'A Consideration', p. 160.

10. 'A Consideration', p. 161.

11. 'A Consideration', p. 167.

subsequently *added* to a psalm. This remains a possibility which, if the final redactors of the Psalter are perhaps to be identified with the authors of the wisdom psalms, needs to be explored; it is a question that has been raised by other scholars.[12]

C. Westermann put forward an important proposal for the interpretation of the Psalter as a whole.[13] He found in Psalms 1 and 119 a clear indication of a major change from the cultic understanding of the Psalms to a treatment of them as a book to be read, studied and meditated on, arguing that these two psalms were added to the collection at a late—though not the final—stage of compilation with precisely this intention. They were not psalms in the strict sense but were intended to constitute a framework to the whole body of psalms, giving it the character of a manual of piety based on the central concept of the Law. At that stage Psalms 1–119 comprised the entire Psalter. Westermann argued that the Psalms, which had originally been expressions of prayer, had now come to be regarded as God's word to humanity. When later the Psalter was completed in its final form, the addition of doxologies at the conclusion of the five Books (Pss. 41, 72, 89, 106, 150) gave it the character of a celebration of God's gracious dealings with humanity. Psalms of praise were also appended to some of the minor collections.

In 1979 B.S. Childs expressed a view similar to that of Westermann.[14] He argued that Psalms 1, 119 and some others, especially 19.9-15, are not to be seen simply as 'spontaneous musings or uncontrolled aspirations, but rather as an answer to God's word, which continues to address Israel in his torah'.[15] Psalm 1 points forward to the Psalter as the medium through which Israel now responds to that word. Further, 'Because Israel continues to hear God's word through the voice of the psalmist's response, these prayers now function as the divine word itself... The study of the Psalter serves as a guidebook along the path of blessing.'[16] Psalm 1 actually specifies that this blessing is mediated

12. This seems to be suggested by I. Engnell, 'The Book of Psalms', in J.T. Willis and H. Ringgren (eds.), *Critical Essays on the Old Testament* (London: SPCK, 1970), p. 99, in an article that has been unjustly neglected.

13. C. Westermann, 'Zur Sammlung des Psalters', *Theologia Viatorum* 8 (1962), pp. 278-84 (= *Forschung am alten Testament* [TBAT, 24; Munich: Chr. Kaiser Verlag, 1964], pp. 336-43).

14. B.S. Childs, *Introduction to the Old Testament as Scripture* (London: SCM Press, 1979), pp. 508-23.

15. *Introduction*, p. 513.

16. *Introduction*, p. 513.

partly through meditation on God's word. The title of the book, *t^e^hillîm*, 'songs of praise', testifies to the fact that the voice is that of Israel, 'but it is only an echo of the divine voice which called his people into being'.

Reindl agreed in many respects with the views of Westermann and Childs, but was more specific about the identity of the final compilers of the Psalter, and he also put forward some more detailed proposals with regard to its compilation.[17] He believed that the Psalter must have been compiled in the Second Temple, but not by temple singers. It was the work of practitioners of wisdom who were the successors of the pre-exilic 'wise men' and, in a sense, the predecessors of Ben Sira. Their piety was centred on the Torah, and they regarded those who did not accept their type of piety as the ungodly. Psalms 1 and 150 show that it was their intention to create the Psalter as a unified whole. They were not, however, opposed to the continued practice of the traditional cult, and in fact their choice of material deliberately catered for the needs of some—but not all—groups other than their own.

Reindl regarded Psalm 1 not as a true psalm but as a wisdom poem (*weisheitliche Lehrdichtung*) composed by a wisdom teacher for his pupils to encourage them in the right way. The word *tôrâ* in Ps. 1.2 identifies the Psalter itself as divine teaching, to be studied (in distinction from the cultic use of the Psalms) day and night. Reindl claimed that there are clear signs that these compilers made changes to many of the psalms, adapting, supplementing and reordering them as well as including psalms of their own composition or others that expressed their own kind of piety. Sections were added to Psalms 50 (v. 16a), 104 (v. 35) and 146 (v. 9b) among others. Certain psalms were placed together as pairs or small groups (105 and 106; 111 and 112; 90–92). Psalms 146–149 were reordered to lead up to the final Psalm 150. Other psalms were also reordered to establish links with adjacent psalms. The intention of the whole was to create a book that combined emphasis on the Torah with praise.

Many of these suggestions had been made by earlier scholars. But in the 1980s and 1990s a number of scholars have pursued in new ways the questions both of the arrangement of psalms and the intentions of the Psalter's final editors. G.H. Wilson in particular made a systematic

17. J. Reindl, 'Weisheitliche Bearbeitung von Psalmen: Ein Beitrag zum Verständnis der Sammlung des Psalters', in J.A. Emerton (ed.), *Congress Volume, Vienna, 1980* (VTSup, 32; Leiden: Brill, 1981), pp. 333-56.

attempt to show that the Psalter in its final form offers evidence of being a single, purposefully edited work.[18]

In his article of 1984 Wilson discussed various techniques employed by editors to group psalms together and also to mark divisions between groups. He found that in Books I–III (Pss. 3–89) there was a concern to group psalms by supposed authorship (David, Korahites, Asaphites) as indicated in the superscriptions (sometimes called titles or headings). The superscriptions also included indications of genre (*mizmôr*, *miktām*, *šîr*, *maśkîl* etc.) which served similar purposes. These devices were not employed systematically, however, and there are numerous exceptions. Wilson further noted that demarcation by superscription was not applied in cases where there is an obvious thematic grouping, such as psalms of divine kingship and royal psalms. With regard to Books IV–V he observed that the grouping techniques employed are different from those employed in Books I–III. The former have very few authorial superscriptions and make little use of genre indications; however, the occurrence of 'hallelujah' at the beginning of a psalm, and also of the phrase 'Give thanks to Yahweh for he is good; his steadfast love endures for ever' or the like sometimes served as grouping techniques. These differences of technique in the editing of these two parts of the Psalter might suggest that Books I–III once constituted a single book to which Books IV–V were subsequently added.

In *The Editing of the Hebrew Psalter* (1985) Wilson followed up these points in greater detail, and adduced further arguments in favour of the view that the Psalter bears the marks of editorial organization. He pointed out that a concern for meaningful arrangement of comparable material is by no means unparalleled in ancient Near Eastern literature, and cited in particular the example of the Sumerian temple hymns, in which various organizational techniques were employed, and in which there is evidence, as in the Hebrew psalms, of the adaptation of psalms away from their original functions to make them conform to the religious fashions and spiritual needs of later generations. Wilson also considered the evidence of the Qumran Psalms manuscripts; these testify to a

18. G.H. Wilson, 'Evidence of Editorial Divisions in the Hebrew Psalter', *VT* 34 (1984), pp. 337-52; *The Editing of the Hebrew Psalter* (SBLDS, 76; Chico, CA: Scholars Press, 1985); 'The Use of Royal Psalms at the "Seams" of the Hebrew Psalter', *JSOT* 35 (1986), pp. 85-94; 'The Shape of the Book of Psalms', *Int* 46 (1992), pp. 129-42.

degree of fluidity in consecutive arrangement, but their fragmentary character makes it impossible to formulate conclusions about a possible alternative Psalter at Qumran.

Wilson here extended his earlier list of editorial techniques employed in the Hebrew Psalter, having noted the almost total absence of *explicit* statements in the text of the Psalter itself pointing to an organizational intention: only once—in Ps. 72.20 ('The prayers of David son of Jesse are ended')—is any such statement to be found. Furthermore, the superscriptions, unlike colophons and similar devices in other ancient Near Eastern literature, served only a limited structural purpose (although they provide evidence of radical reinterpretation of some psalms): they are not the work of the final editor, and thus do not provide evidence of the organization of the whole Psalter. The investigator is therefore obliged to rely wholly on the *implicit* evidence of the texts. Relevant techniques, apart from those already mentioned by Wilson, include the formation of pairs of psalms by the device of placing an untitled psalm immediately after a related titled one, grouping by identical or similar incipits (a device employed in the Sumerian temple psalm collections), use of key phrases, the separate grouping of 'Elohist' psalms, doxologies and hallelujah psalms.

Wilson's analysis, thorough though it is, is thus mainly concerned with indications of lesser groupings of psalms that preceded the final editing of the Psalter as an integral work. One of Wilson's main arguments for the unity of the book, however, concerns the character and placing of Psalm 1. In seeing this psalm as having been deliberately placed in order to constitute an introduction to the whole Psalter, Wilson followed Westermann, Childs and Reindl. He characterized this psalm as providing the readers with 'hermeneutical spectacles' through which to view the Psalter as a whole and meditate on it, seeking for themselves the will of God as expressed in the Torah. Confirmation that the Psalter was intended by the editors to be used in this way was to be found in the 'historical' superscriptions that refer to incidents in the life of David. Through these superscriptions the readers were encouraged to find models for their own righteous behaviour in accordance with the Torah and to acquire a trust in God comparable with that of David when encountering personal situations comparable to his.

A novel feature of Wilson's work was his stress on the importance of discovering the 'seams' that join together various groups of psalms and which thus created the unity of the book. One reason for the need to devise such 'seams' was that the freedom of the final editor to carry out his organizational scheme was limited by the existence of already formed groups of psalms which he could not or did not wish to break up, and which therefore had to be incorporated into his scheme.

To the final editor's intention Wilson devoted only a short section of his book. He considered this in terms of the divisions between the five Books (which he did not connect with the liturgical reading of the five books of the Pentateuch). Books I–III (Pss. 3–89) were primarily concerned with David, the covenant with David and the failure of the promise to David's descendants, and Book IV (Pss. 90–106) with the implications of that failure and the problems raised by it. Book V offers an answer to the plight of the exiles and their plea for help, offering new hope through the portrayal of the kingship of Yahweh who fully deserves universal praise. In his 1992 article Wilson offered alternative theories of the motive behind the organization of the Psalter. From Brueggemann he took the notion that the Psalter moves from the call to obedience to the call to praise; from Childs, the emphasis on the fact that according to Psalm 1 the Torah is not a burden but a delight and the observation that the Psalms, which had originally been expressions of prayer *to* God, had in their final shape come to be regarded as God's word of revelation to humanity. In this article Wilson discerned not one but two overriding themes: that of David and the covenant, and that of wisdom. But his suggestion that in the second half of the Psalter there is a shift from the individual to the collective is disconcerting. Such an interpretation militates against Wilson's earlier view that the whole Psalter has been arranged as a manual of private devotion with Psalm 1 as its introduction, and indeed against the whole idea of its redactional unity. Against his view it may be argued that although many of the psalms in the second half of the Psalter are addressed to or written from the point of view of a community rather than a single individual, this is due to their original function rather than to their new role. Throughout the Psalter there are many psalms in which the individual worshipper—who in fact would always have been very aware of his or her solidarity with the people as a whole—had to read 'I' for 'we', in the same way that, in the David psalms, an individual could put himself or herself into the place of another. The communal character, for example, of the psalms of praise at the conclusion of the Psalter need have presented no problem to the individual Israelite who used them for private meditations and silent acts of praise, and cannot be said, in terms of the role of the

Psalter that is under discussion here, to represent a shift from the individual to the collective.

An interesting variant of the notion of the non-cultic use of the Psalms came from the literary critic R. Alter.[19] Alter's view is of particular interest because it is very close to that of Gunkel, who seventy years earlier regarded many, if not most, of the psalms as 'spiritual songs' composed by and for pious individuals to sing, but which had preserved the forms and language of the official Israelite cult. Alter took a similar view: he did not speak of the *reinterpretation* of cultic psalms by teachers of individual piety, but stressed the power of metaphor in poetry, suggesting that in these psalms the cultic language may have been intended in a metaphorical sense from the outset: in other words, that many of them were never used in the public cult at all.

Psalm 73 stands at the central point of the 150 psalms; it also introduces Book III of the Psalter. In an article of 1987 McCann suggested that this psalm marks a turning point theologically as well.[20] He argued that it is indeed a microcosm of Old Testament theology. In the context of the whole Psalter it epitomizes a tension between the problem of the suffering of the faithful (vv. 1-12) and their loyalty to traditional beliefs, and offers a solution (vv. 18-28), with vv. 13-17 as the pivotal point in terms of a personal struggle which is resolved in a recognition that it is possible to endure pain and suffering while yet remaining faithful to the traditional notions of suffering as a punishment for sin. It revolutionizes the concept of the 'pure in heart' as 'those who continue to obey, serve and praise God even while stricken and troubled'.[21] This singling out of Psalm 73 as a pivotal psalm supports the notion of a progressive theological development in the total structure of the Psalter.

J.L. Mays, in his Presidential Address to the Society of Biblical Literature in 1986,[22] named the three 'Torah psalms' as containing the central clue to the interpretation of the Psalter in its final form, and also

19. R. Alter, 'Psalms', in Alter and F. Kermode (eds.), *The Literary Guide to the Bible* (London: Collins, 1987), pp. 244-62.

20. J.C. McCann, Jr, 'Psalm 73: A Microcosm of Old Testament Theology', in K.G. Hoglund *et al.* (eds.), *The Listening Heart: Essays in Wisdom and the Psalms in Honor of Roland E. Murphy, O. Carm* (JSOTSup, 58; Sheffield: JSOT Press, 1987), pp. 247-57.

21. McCann, 'Psalm 73', pp. 251-52.

22. J.L. Mays, 'The Place of the Torah-Psalms in the Psalter', *JBL* 106 (1987), pp. 3-12.

identified 14 other psalms scattered through the book as conveying the same message. The whole Psalter was to be read in the light of their principles: it was to be seen as a non-sacrificial 'liturgy' whose constant recital would lead beyond meditation to action: to the thinking, willing and doing of God's will. Mays made no specific suggestion about the overall structure of the Psalter; but he drew attention to certain instances where the pairing of psalms was intended to emphasize Israel's eschatological hope.

Brueggemann was wholly concerned with the 'theological intentionality' of the Psalter.[23] For him, the fixed points were Psalms 1, 73 and 150. The theological progression—'how one gets from one end of the Psalter to the other'—can be summed up as a progression from obedience to praise. Both Psalm 1 and Psalm 150 are 'innocent'—that is, they are confident and untroubled. But the 'innocence' of Psalm 150 is very different from that of Psalm 1. The latter expresses a simple confidence that the righteous will flourish through their obedience and that the wicked will fade away; its intention is to facilitate a new interpretation of the succeeding psalms in terms of a trusting, joyous community. While they recognize that the real world involves suffering and so often calls for lament, the hymns hold out the hope and trust that the suffering will be overcome through faith and obedience. Psalm 73 (here Brueggemann picked up the insights of McCann and Wilson) marks a transition: it moves beyond the simple faith expressed in Psalm 1 to a recognition that God's presence and communion with him that are available to the worshipper outweigh all concern about the prosperity of the wicked. God's *ḥesed*, which had seemed to be a matter of doubt in some of the preceding psalms, is seen to be the true reality and is fully satisfying (vv. 23-26). Finally, in Psalm 150, there is a totally confident outburst of praise of God which has become possible because the lessons of life have been learned. Even the duty of obedience taught by Psalm 1 no longer needs to be mentioned because it has been swallowed up in unalloyed joy in the presence of God.

McCann followed up his earlier study of Psalm 73 and Wilson's work on Psalms 19 and 119 with a consideration of other types of psalm that appear to have been placed in their present positions not haphazardly but as crucial elements in the editorial reorientation of the Psalms as

23. W. Brueggemann, 'Bounded by Obedience and Praise: The Psalms as Canon', *JSOT* 50 (1991), pp. 63-92.

instruction.[24] Thus immediately after Psalm 1, which 'invites the reader to receive what follows as instruction',[25] Psalm 2 'introduces the essential content which the Psalter intends to teach—that the Lord reigns!'[26] This affirmation is then taken up again at the end of Book II in Psalm 72 and at the end of Book III in Psalm 89. The theme is then further reinforced in Book IV in the enthronement psalms 93 and 95–99, 'which became the theological "heart" of the expanded final Psalter'.[27] By this proclamation of God's reign the Psalter calls people to a decision. The hymns, which conclude in the final verse of Psalm 150 with the words 'Let everything that breathes praise the Lord!', stress the universality of praise, which is not simply a liturgical act but the goal of all human life. The laments, in their movement from complaint to trust, also exemplify the grace of God which operates through and despite the agony of life's experiences. (It may be remarked that in part McCann's article is more concerned to show what the Psalms can teach *us* than to illuminate the actual intentions of the final editors of the Psalter—perhaps it shows a tendency to overstate a promising theme.)

M.S. Smith found a coherent theology in the work of the final redactors of the Psalter, one which was essentially eschatological.[28] In Books I–III the compilers presented the historical David in their own terms—that is, as the composer of psalms, as the organizer of the temple liturgy, and as one who had experienced God's faithfulness to his covenant. Books IV–V move the perspective from the past to the present and the future, placing all hopes for the returned exiles on the divine king, Yahweh, who will restore the nation and establish a *new* David, the messianic king. This argument is based on two kinds of evidence: the superscriptions and the royal psalms. Smith noted that whereas in Books I and II the superscriptions concerning David interpret these psalms in terms of the historical David (the Korah and Asaph psalms in Book III being also associated with him as the organizer, with Solomon, of the temple liturgy), the David superscriptions in Books IV and V no longer refer to the historical David: it is to the coming 'new' David that they refer. Book IV, which begins with the Songs of Ascents whose superscriptions refer to the return from exile, puts forward the preconditions

24. J.C. McCann, Jr, 'The Psalms as Instruction', *Int* 46 (1992), pp. 117-28.
25. McCann, 'The Psalms as Instruction', p. 119.
26. McCann, 'The Psalms as Instruction', p. 123.
27. McCann, 'The Psalms as Instruction', p. 123, quoting Wilson.
28. M.S. Smith, 'The Psalms as a Book for Pilgrims', *Int* 46 (1992), pp. 156-66.

for the manifestation of *divine* kingship. But the royal psalms in Books I–III (2, 72, 89) may already have been given an eschatological construction. This is certainly the case with Psalm 110 in Book V: the royal figure there is presented in terms strikingly different from the others.

From the books and articles discussed so far it is apparent that new ways of approaching the Psalter have been placed firmly on the agenda of Psalms studies. A recent series of further contributions to the subject is to be found in a 1993 collection of essays entitled *The Shape and Shaping of the Psalter*[29] by a group of scholars of whom the majority had made earlier contributions (discussed above). This volume arose mainly from discussions in the Psalms Group of the Society of Biblical Literature; most of the essays owe their origins to meetings of the Group since 1989. They are intended to offer refinements of earlier work and to explore further the theological implications of the new approach. They will be briefly considered below.

Mays, continuing his thesis of the Psalter as instruction, offered new reflections on the Torah psalms.[30] He considered that the interpretation of the Psalms as instruction began relatively early. It is not only to be found in late psalms composed for this purpose but is also an integral feature of much older psalms. Only with the final redaction of the Psalter was the instructional motive applied to the whole collection. Citing Psalm 73 as an example of a hymn specifically composed with a clear intention to instruct, he suggested that all types of psalm have a potential pedagogical intention because they speak about God, world and self. The aim of the final redactor was to bring out this potential in the Psalter as a whole. There was thus a continuity between the older and the new psalmody. Mays did not entirely agree with the view that the final redactors aimed to create a handbook for individual silent meditation. Rather, the stress on instruction had opened the way to a variety of possible uses which could have included a corporate or communal use.

Murphy, in replying to Mays's initial question 'Is it possible and useful to read a psalm as part of the book of Psalms, to understand it under the directives furnished by the book as a whole?', a question that Mays had clearly answered in the affirmative, sounded a note of caution

29. J.C. McCann, Jr (ed.), *The Shape and Shaping of the Psalter* (JSOTSup, 159; Sheffield: JSOT Press, 1993).

30. J.L. Mays, 'The Question of Context in Psalm Interpretation', in McCann (ed.), *Shape and Shaping*, pp. 14-20.

with regard to the whole enterprise.[31] Noting that Mays's contextual approach to the Psalms is no less hypothetical than other interpretations, he called for the establishing of sound criteria. There was a danger, he argued, that uncontrolled pursuit of these theories might end in anarchy. He cited examples—such as the hypothesis of Psalms 1 and 2 having been linked together as an introduction to the Psalter—where the alleged evidence was too slender to justify the conclusions that had been drawn. Murphy found the contextual approach to be in many cases less helpful to the reader than meditation on particular psalms in isolation, and proposed that the 'historical literal meaning' of a psalm should be the basis for its further study, though the various approaches, including contextual interpretation, should be given consideration.

Brueggemann, also in response to Mays's article, raised important theological questions arising from it.[32] He questioned the alleged contrast which had originated with Gunkel and Mowinckel between 'cultic' and 'non-cultic', and declared himself uneasy about the notion of 'book in context', suggesting the alternative of 'history in context'. He saw cult not in terms of Mowinckel's idea of it but in much broader terms, a s 'the matrix of symbolism by which the community continuously reasserts its identity and reconstructs its life'.[33] In this sense all the psalms are cultic. The Psalter bears the marks of a necessary historical adjustment of Israel's life in a Persian or Hellenistic environment; but there was continuity, not a complete break. Brueggemann reaffirmed his view of a progression within the Psalter which recorded a movement from lament and complaint through faith and trust to praise and thanksgiving; but this was a literary phenomenon, the outcome of the historical adjustment that the new circumstances had led the community to make, rather than the creation of a purely pedagogical handbook.

The remaining articles in this volume illustrate the complexity of the new type of Psalms study and the variety of possible approaches and aims. G.H. Wilson was especially concerned with the question of editorial links between individual psalms and small groups of psalms, and with the possibility that the whole Psalter is the product of a 'systematic, purposeful and theologically motivated arrangement of

31. R.E. Murphy, 'Reflections on Contextual Interpretation of the Psalms', in McCann (ed.), *Shape and Shaping*, pp. 21-28.

32. W. Brueggemann, 'Response to James L. Mays, "The Question of Context"', in McCann (ed.), *Shape and Shaping*, pp. 29-41.

33. Brueggemann, 'Response', p. 31.

individual psalms', but cautioned against the making of superficial and inadequately argued conclusions.[34] D.M. Howard, Jr, attempted a progress report.[35] He noted that work up to date had proceeded on two distinct levels: on a higher level, the postulation of 'large, organizing principles' and, on a lower level, the investigation of links between adjacent psalms. These complement each other, however, to the extent that the former provides a context for the latter. With regard to the latter, he asserted (with tongue in cheek?) that 'if work at the lower level continues very long, every pair of adjacent psalms will be shown to have significant—or logical—links between them' (cf. Murphy's warning against carrying a thesis too far), which would no doubt, if demonstrated, confirm the work done at the higher level.

Both of the other contributors to the volume concentrated on the general editorial purpose of the Psalter. P.D. Miller pursued further the theme of Psalms 1 and 2 together serving as an introduction to the whole Psalter—a thesis emphatically rejected by Murphy—though he confined his arguments almost entirely to Books I–III.[36] McCann began by remarking that the investigation has been pursued not on two but on several fronts: the re-reading of individual psalms to provide a new interpretation for the post-exilic community, the investigation of links between adjacent psalms, and the study of the final form and editorial purpose of the entire Psalter.[37] An additional aspect not mentioned by him is the interpretation of the Psalter as a handbook for individual devotion. McCann followed Wilson's proposal to investigate the 'seams' between the Books, and concluded that the essential purpose of the Psalter was to address the problems posed by the failure of the Davidic monarchy and the exile and dispersion that followed. The Psalter addresses the needs of a whole community—a view that McCann recognized as standing in tension (but, he claimed, a fruitful tension) with the emphasis placed by Childs and others on the Psalter as intended

34. G.H. Wilson, 'Understanding the Purposeful Arrangement of Psalms in the Psalter: Pitfalls and Promise'; 'Shaping the Psalter: A Consideration of Editorial Linkage in the Book of Psalms', in McCann (ed.), *Shape and Shaping*, pp. 42-51; 72-82.

35. D.M. Howard, Jr, 'Editorial Activity in the Psalter: A State-of-the-Field Survey', in McCann (ed.), *Shape and Shaping*, pp. 52-70.

36. P.D. Miller, Jr, 'The Beginning of the Psalter', in McCann (ed.), *Shape and Shaping*, pp. 83-92.

37. J.C. McCann, Jr, 'Books I–III and the Editorial Purpose of the Hebrew Psalter', in *idem* (ed.), *Shape and Shaping*, pp. 93-107.

to encourage individuals to appropriate for themselves the lessons implicit in the psalmists' exposition of the struggles in their inner lives. The articles in this volume sometimes give the impression of reworking arguments that had already been put forward by the contributors or by others, and apart from some clarification of the issues it is doubtful whether it can be said that they make a significant advance in the discussion of the subject.

The most recent and ambitious contribution to the debate about the composition of the Psalter is that of M. Millard.[38] Millard claims that the Psalter provides enough internal evidence to make it possible to trace in detail the whole process of the Psalter's composition from the formation of pairs of psalms to the completed work, and also to determine the chronology of that process. Every one of the 150 psalms is treated in his analysis, and every one is duly docketed.

Millard is right to make use of a variety of kinds of evidence to further his argument, though he finds some more useful than others. The superscriptions attached to some psalms are held to be important evidence, as also are style and language; but Millard is somewhat sceptical of arguments based on chiastic patterns as employed by Auffret and others to define groups of psalms, and also of those based on key words (*Stichworte*); in particular, the repetition of such words is too frequent throughout the Psalter to be used as conclusive proof of links between adjacent psalms, except in a few cases.

Millard holds that the Psalter is 'post-cultic', in that it is a book of prayers rather than a collection designed for public use in the Jerusalem temple. His view that it is to a large extent a product of the Diaspora is an interesting one. He sees this post-cultic character as having begun to be evident already in the Second Temple stage of development, and holds that a large number of the psalms—not only the Songs of Ascents—are pilgrimage psalms expressing the longing of Diaspora Jews to visit the distant temple. Nevertheless, he uses evidence from postbiblical sources to show that the Psalter did *not* become the normative official Jewish prayer book (as it did in Christian usage), because it was too long to be so used, and also too repetitious. Copies may have been owned, after its canonization, by some families; but its actual private use was eclectic, selected psalms being used as prayers in the family, especially at times of crisis or distress.

38. M. Millard, *Die Komposition des Psalters* (Forschungen zum Alten Testament, 9; Tübingen: Mohr, 1994).

Millard makes a number of valid points, especially with regard to form-critical matters. In particular, he uses recent views about the internal unity of some psalms to draw conclusions about the formation of groups. Pointing out that within a single psalm changes of *Gattung*, number (singular to plural and vice versa) and persons addressed are no longer regarded as proving literary disunity, he argues by analogy that this is also true, *mutatis mutandis*, of sequences of adjacent psalms: abrupt changes of *Gattung*, for example, from lament to praise from one psalm to the next should not be seen as indications of random juxtaposition, but may point to a deliberate arrangement made in order to create a progressive movement of thought and feeling. Such a movement might, and frequently does, mark a progress from lament to praise, often mediated by an intervening divine oracle of reassurance.

The main weakness of Millard's argument lies in the fact that the evidences of composition are too sparse and too ambiguous to support his contentions. This is true both of his reconstruction of the process of composition of individual psalms and of his attempts to link the supposed stages in a chronological scheme. Frequently his dating of the composition of individual psalms as well as of their insertion into their present contexts appears arbitrary and even bizarre, as when, for example, he categorizes the so-called 'entrance psalms' 15 and 24 as 'post-cultic'. Such judgments appear to have been made in order to fit a predetermined scheme. Again, Millard fails to deal convincingly with psalms that appear incongruous in their present settings, such as Psalm 45. Millard's hypotheses, then, must be judged to go beyond the available evidence.

Points of Agreement

On many points there has been a general agreement, at least implicitly, among those recent scholars who have discussed the composition and purpose of the Psalter.

1. It was generally agreed that the Psalter is not a random collection of psalms but was designed to constitute, in some sense, a coherent book.
2. It was agreed that the Psalms, most of which were originally cultic—that is, composed for use in various kinds of public worship—were given a new interpretation in the post-exilic period. Evidence of this is to be found *inter alia* in the addition

of superscriptions to many psalms, the inclusion in the book of psalms that do not appear to have originated in the cult, and the significant placing of Psalm 1.

3. While the Jerusalem temple continued to function, the new understanding of the Psalter was not necessarily opposed to the traditional cultic usage, but was intended to offer an alternative way of using the Psalms in the new circumstances of the post-exilic period.
4. The positioning of certain psalms (other than Ps. 1) is crucial for the study of the structure and theological meaning of the Psalter.
5. There is evidence that some pairs and small groups of psalms were formed by the redactors in order to further the new interpretation.
6. Groups of psalms already formed at an earlier time were retained by the final redactors.
7. The psalms, most of which were expressions of prayer, came to be regarded as a source of instruction or an aid to theological reflection (God's word to humanity).

Disputed Matters

While there has been general agreement that the final arrangement of the Psalter was made under the influence of a significantly changed view of the nature and purpose of the Psalms, there has been no consensus of opinion regarding the precise uses to which the compilers intended the Psalter to be put, or regarding the process of its composition. Some scholars (such as Mays) suggested that its compilation opened the way to a variety of new uses. That this might be so was not denied by any of the scholars mentioned above; nevertheless different emphases were placed on this.

1. Some scholars (especially Westermann and Childs) argued that the Psalter was primarily intended to be a spiritual guide or handbook directing the piety of individuals who read it and meditated on it silently and in private.
2. Some (especially Wilson) argued that the Psalter was intended for use—presumably public recitation—by the community. This appears to imply public worship of some kind, and, for some (such as Brueggemann) raised the question of the character of the post-exilic cult.

3. Some (especially Wilson) argued that the Psalter was intended as a manual of instruction. This is a variation on the concept of meditation; but instruction could take the form either of *self*-instruction by individuals or the instruction of a group by a teacher.
4. Little if any progress has been made as to the identity of the final compilers of the Psalter. This is due to a remarkable paucity of information available to the scholar both about the general religious situation and about temple worship in the post-exilic or Second Temple period to which the compilation of the Psalter has been generally assigned.
5. The frequency of laments and of Davidic psalms at the beginning of the Psalter and of hymns of praise at the end suggested that the Psalter may have been intended to chronicle a progression of thought; but whether this is purely theological (for instance, from a call to obedience to a call to praise) or literary-historical (reflecting on the failure of the Davidic dynasty, then on the perplexity of post-exilic developments and finally leading to a renewal of confidence in Yahweh's sovereignty) was not agreed.
6. The degree to which the Psalter should be regarded as a totally integrated and systematically ordered work was not clearly affirmed by some scholars (such as Miller), whose studies have been mainly confined to particular portions of it.

Differences of Method

Recent studies have been pursued on different levels and by different approaches.

1. Some scholars have approached the subject by looking for ways in which adjacent psalms may be linked by language, theme or logic, while others have looked for signs of a theological or thematic *movement* or progression embracing the Psalter as a whole. These approaches are not *a priori* incompatible, but it is not (yet) clear how they can be meaningfully integrated.
2. Apart from Psalms 1 and 150, on which there has been a substantial agreement, a variety of different suggestions have been put forward about those psalms that have the greatest

significance as structural markers for the Psalter as a whole. Among those proposed are Psalms 2, 19, 72, 73 and 119. Whether it is possible to combine these suggestions into a single theory remains to be seen. The possible significance of the juxtaposition of Psalms 1 and 2 has been discussed but no agreement has been reached.

3. There has been no agreement on the specific grouping of psalms by the final or the penultimate editors.
4. The significance of the superscriptions is disputed. It has been suggested that they are not the work of the final editors but were added at an early stage or stages.

Finally, some contributors to the discussion (notably Murphy and Wilson) have urged caution, referring to the necessarily speculative nature of the enterprise (this is, of course, also true of much of the earlier study of the Psalms, at least since Mowinckel), pointing out the danger of uncontrolled speculation and stressing the need for the establishment of criteria. It is not clear that such criteria have been agreed upon.

Further Progress?

If some of the conclusions summarized above may be correct, is it possible to find further evidence to support them? Can we take such evidence for granted? Some general observations are in order here.

I have already cited D.M. Howard's assertion that, if research into the pairing of adjacent psalms continues to be carried out, soon 'every pair of adjacent psalms will be shown to have some significant...links between them'. Whether he anticipates that such a result is possible is not clear; such a tight organization of disparate literary material would be unique in the ancient world; it has even proved to be beyond the powers of the compilers of modern hymn books. That there are links between certain pairs of adjacent psalms is probable, even certain; but, whatever purpose the Psalter may have been intended to serve, it is inconceivable that it could yield the kind of evidence anticipated by Howard. Something much more modest is all that can be expected along these lines; and it is in fact questionable whether progress is possible beyond what has already been proved or proposed. But what has in fact been proved?

There is a need to reconsider the view that the Psalter demonstrates the existence of a spiritual or theological scheme in which there is a deliberate movement from lament to triumphant praise, from obedience to praise, or the like. The only part of that theory that can be objectively substantiated is that the Psalter *ends* with an expression of pure praise. Here there are no exceptions or doubtful cases: the last five psalms all begin and end with the term 'hallelujah', 'Praise the Lord', and all praise God and thank him for the benefits that he has conferred and still confers on humanity. There can be no doubt at all that these psalms have been deliberately assembled to form a group; and the fact that the Psalter thus concludes on a sustained note of praise cannot be a coincidence.

Matters are far less clear, however, with regard to the beginning of the Psalter. It cannot be said that a single theme exclusively dominates Psalms 1–41, though there is reason to suppose that these psalms at one time formed a separate collection. They conclude with a doxology (Ps. 41.14) as do the other Books. But there is reason to doubt whether the compiler of Book I had any definite scheme in mind. Though psalms of lamentation predominate in this collection, at least 16 psalms are of quite different character, even though some of these contain elements of appeals for help. Nor is it possible to find any system governing the choice of superscriptions. Of these psalms, 34 are attributed to David, but many of these are not lamentations; only four (Pss. 3, 7, 18, 34) are associated with events in the life of David and could perhaps be interpreted by readers as models of behaviour in adversity. Two psalms are connected with cultic occasions; some others have superscriptions with information about types of psalm, musical directions and the like. It is consequently difficult to characterize this group except as showing exceptional interest in David (though in fact the superscription *l^e^dāwīd* does not necessarily refer to the historical David).

But if the kind of theological or spiritual movement throughout the Psalter that has been postulated is to be demonstrated, the crucial Books are II–IV. It is doubtful whether such a demonstration is possible. It is true that there are some observable differences between some of these Books. Book II (Pss. 42–72), however, does not differ greatly in content from Book I: the 31 psalms in this Book include 22 ascriptions to David, including eight whose superscriptions refer to incidents in his life, though seven psalms are attributed to the sons of Korah and one to Asaph. The 16 laments or appeals to God for help are almost all individual.

The 17 psalms in Book III (Pss. 73–89) mark a change in that only one (Ps. 86) is attributed to David, again an individual lament; almost all the others are attributed to Asaph. In five of the eight laments, however, the psalmist speaks of the community ('we'). Both Books II and III contain a few examples of hymns of praise (five in Book II, four in Book III). This feature is almost entirely lacking in Book I.

Book IV (Pss. 90–106) has relatively few superscriptions (seven), only two laments, one individual (Ps. 102) and one communal (Ps. 90), but contains five hymns of praise in addition to the six that celebrate the kingship of Yahweh (Pss. 93, 95–99). Only two are attributed to David.

Of the 44 psalms in Book V there are no less than 20 hymns or psalms of praise, which include twelve hallelujah psalms mainly arranged in groups (Pss. 111–113, 115–117, 146–150); the 15 Songs of Ascents (Pss. 120–134) also belong here. Rather surprisingly there is once again a series of 14 psalms attributed to David, including the consecutive group Psalms 138–145. Whether this is a 'new' David viewed differently from the 'old' David, however, is speculative: the same superscription *l^e^dāwīd* is employed as in Book I. There are no lamentations.

It is clear, therefore, that the Psalter begins with an emphasis (though not an exclusive one) on lament and ends on a note of praise. But it is less clear that between Books I and V there is a significant progression from one to the other in thought or mood that would support the notion of an all-embracing structure for the book as a whole. Further, the positions of the so-called 'Torah' and 'Wisdom' psalms, which are scattered throughout the Psalter, do not chronicle such a movement, although it is true that the 'central' Psalm 73 which begins Book III could be understood as in some sense indicating the way in which despair could be overcome and hope restored, and that the occurrence of the Yahweh-*mālāk* psalms in Book IV might have been intended to herald the mood of praise that pervades Book V.

One of the main difficulties in attempting to understand the redaction of the Psalter lies in the evident complexity of the process of its composition. Millard's efforts to trace each stage from the simple pairing of psalms through the gradual formation of groups and sections of the book to the completed work, and to discover the motives lying behind each stage, certainly point to that complexity, but remain speculative; by the same token, to attempt to determine which features of the book are to be attributed to the final redaction rather than to some earlier one is equally speculative. All that can be done is to examine the Psalter as it stands in its final form and to seek in its contents some clues as to its character and intention.

Chapter 2

WISDOM AND TORAH MATERIAL

As we have seen, a prominent theme of recent discussion has been the occurrence of wisdom and Torah psalms and their significance for the understanding of the structure and composition of the Psalter. The relationship between wisdom piety and the Torah piety of the late post-exilic period was a close one although the two are not identical. Ben Sira, writing in the early second century BCE, stated that the two streams had become one: obedience to the teaching of Wisdom, who proceeds from the mouth of God (Sir. 24.3) is not to be distinguished from the written Torah (Sir. 24.23). In later Judaism the Torah became the central feature of the Jewish faith. In the Psalter the Torah psalms (Pss. 1, 119; see below on Ps. 19) and the wisdom psalms still retain their respective characteristics: while the former concern themselves exclusively with obedience to and meditation on the written Torah, the latter range more widely, retaining the character of traditional wisdom in that they concern themselves with such matters as faith and doubt (see for example Ps. 73) and with the meaning of human existence and the place of humanity within the created universe (see for example Ps. 8). Both types of psalm, however, stand out thematically from the generality of the Psalms, and in general present the same problems for the composition of the Psalter; they may therefore be considered together. Further consideration of their role is needed, and the pages that follow will be devoted to this subject.

Torah psalms are not difficult to define. But with regard to the definition of a wisdom psalm, as shown by the above discussions, no agreement has been reached. The number of psalms that have been so defined is very large, but the criteria are not clear cut, and no two scholars have been entirely in agreement in their selection, even when there has been substantial agreement about the criteria.

The first attempt to define the criteria was made by Gunkel.[1] His view

1. *Einleitung in die Psalmen*, pp. 389-97.

that the wisdom poetry of the Old Testament is especially characterized by a didactic intention and the expression of personal and individual experience was widely accepted, but later scholars have added to the list of criteria, citing 'learned' authorship (so Mowinckel, von Rad, Reindl, McCann, Mays), certain stylistic features (Murphy[2]), recurring motifs (Kuntz[3]), a mood of private devotion and piety (G.W. Anderson[4]), a concern for order (Crenshaw[5]), and so on.

Some attempt at definition must evidently be made for the purpose of the present study. Clearly the term 'wisdom psalm'—and this applies also to any passage that may be deemed to be an interpolation into, or a subsequent addition to, a psalm of different type—can only properly be used of a psalm that employs *modes of thought* especially characteristic of the books that are generally recognized as wisdom literature: this means primarily Proverbs, Job and Ecclesiastes as far as the Hebrew Old Testament is concerned. The *literary form* of such psalms is not of the first importance: the wisdom literature employs a number of different forms, and there is no single characteristic form. Some wisdom books use characteristic language or terminology, however, and when this occurs in a psalm it is usually a pointer to its being a wisdom psalm.

An equally clear pointer is a disposition to *reflection*, especially on personal experiences and on the problems and implications of religious faith and of the human condition in general. The didactic element noted by Gunkel is present in some wisdom psalms (though not in all): the writer assumes the role of teacher, often employing terminology characteristic of the specifically didactic parts of the book of Proverbs. Thus a wisdom psalm does not necessarily take the form of a prayer addressed to God, but rather of a lesson addressed to the reader. Its general tone is usually easily distinguishable. Not all these characteristics are present in every wisdom psalm, and there are marginal cases. As stated above, the surest criterion is a general conformity to the concerns of the wisdom literature proper.

The pure wisdom and Torah psalms will be considered below. But in

2. 'A Consideration'.

3. J.K. Kuntz, 'The Retribution Motif in Psalmic Wisdom', *ZAW* 89 (1977), pp. 223-33.

4. G.W. Anderson, '"Sicut Cervus": Evidence in the Psalter of Private Devotion in Ancient Israel', *VT* 30 (1980), pp. 388-97.

5. J.L. Crenshaw, 'Wisdom', in J.H. Hayes (ed.), *Old Testament Form Criticism* (San Antonio: Trinity University Press, 1974), pp. 225-64.

my opinion a question of equal, if not greater, importance is whether and to what extent other older psalms, such as those originally intended for cultic use, may have been reinterpreted or reoriented by means of additions or interpolations in order to make them suitable for devotional or instructional use. In other words, it is important to discover whether there was a *systematic editorial attempt* to convert the collection of Psalms into a wisdom or Torah Psalter. For such a purpose this kind of redactional work would have been essential. It is difficult to believe that the inclusion of a limited number of pure wisdom or Torah psalms scattered in isolated positions in the Psalter could by itself have produced a recognizably wisdom- or Torah-oriented Psalter whose new character would have been obvious to the reader. Some further editorial activity would have been required. This is a consideration that has received minimal attention in recent discussion.

This question will be dealt with as a priority. But before a general investigation of the role of wisdom and Torah material is undertaken, it is necessary to turn our attention to one Torah psalm in particular: Psalm 1.

Psalm 1

The notion that Psalm 1 constitutes an introduction to the Psalter is an ancient one that goes back at least as far as Jerome.[6] But the view expressed in some recent discussion, that it was composed specifically to be a guide to the reading of the Psalter, providing the reader with 'hermeneutical spectacles' (Wilson's term) through which to view the psalms that follow, is comparatively new.

Psalm 1 asserts the certainty of divine blessing and prosperity for the man (*ʾîš*) who avoids the company and the ways of the wicked and sinners (v. 1) and whose 'delight is in the law of Yahweh' (*bᵉtôrat yhwh ḥepṣô*) on which he meditates (*yehgeh*) day and night (v. 2). In much recent discussion it has been taken for granted that the phrase 'the Torah of Yahweh' refers not to the Law of Moses but to the Psalter: that is, that the Psalter is to be the subject of meditation. In view of the multiplicity of senses in which the word *tôrâ* is used in the Old Testament this view needs to be examined. The use of the verb *hāgâ*, 'meditate', strongly suggests—though this is not *certainly* the case—that *tôrâ* in v. 2 refers to an acknowledged written corpus. The meanings 'growl' and 'mutter' for *hāgâ* attested in other Old Testament passages make it probable that

6. See Jacquet, *Les psaumes et le coeur de l'homme*, I, p. 203.

the verb is here to be seen as having retained a vocal sense, that is, of reading aloud—probably by an individual, to himself or herself and in a low tone—as was customary in the ancient world. But what was it that was to be read?

It is significant that in Josh. 1.7-8 Yahweh gives a remarkably similar command to Joshua with regard to his study of the 'book of the Torah':

> This book of the Torah shall not depart out of your mouth; you shall meditate on it day and night (*wᵉhāgîtā bô yômām wālaylâ*), so that you may be careful to act in accordance with all that is written in it. For then you shall make your way prosperous (*taṣlîaḥ 'et-dᵉrākᵉkā)*, and you shall be successful.

The coincidences of vocabulary (*ûbᵉtôrātô yehgeh yômam wālaylâ*, Ps. 1.2; *wᵉhāgîtā bô yômām wālaylâ*, Josh. 1.8; *wᵉkōl ʾᵃšer yaʿᵃśeh yaṣlîaḥ*, Ps. 1.3; *lᵉmaʿan taśkîl bᵉkōl ʾᵃšer tēlēk,* Josh. 1.7; *ʿāz taṣlîaḥ ʾet dᵉrākᵉkā*, Josh. 1.8) can hardly be missed. Somewhat similarly, Deut. 17.18-19, part of the 'law of the king', though it does not employ the verb *hāgâ*, contains a comparable command:

> When he has taken the throne of his kingdom, he shall write (*wᵉkātab lô*) a copy of this law (*hattôrâ hazzōʾt*) in the presence of the levitical priests. It shall remain with him, and he shall read in it (*wᵉqārāʾ bô*) all the days of his life, so that he may learn to fear Yahweh his God.

In both instances the *tôrâ* referred to is the Deuteronomic code of laws.

In the Old Testament the principal meanings of the word *tôrâ* are direction, instruction and law. In the last of these senses, *God's* Torah may denote particular priestly regulations, a group or body of laws, or a specific code of laws, especially that of Deuteronomy or (in Chronicles) the priestly code of laws—that is, the so-called Law of Moses. In the prophetical books the term occurs fairly frequently in the sense of Yahweh's teaching, sometimes in parallel with his justice. But it is never used in the Old Testament of any substantial written corpus except the Law of Moses.[7] If in Ps. 1.2 it denoted the written corpus of the *Psalter* (or if this meaning extended also to Pss. 19 and 119) this would be a unique usage. But there is nothing in the text of these psalms that indicates that this is the case; and as has been suggested above, their most natural interpretation is that they refer to the Law of Moses, possibly to the Code of Deuteronomy or, depending on the date to which these psalms should be attributed, to the priestly laws or to the whole

7. See the article 'Tora' in *THAT*, II, cols. 1032-1043.

Pentateuch. In other words, these psalms reflect the beginning of that intensive study of the law that characterized later Judaism.

Some modern commentators have argued for a much wider interpretation of *tôrâ* in Ps. 1.2. Dahood, for example, maintained that in all three Torah psalms the word *tôrâ* denotes 'law' in the widest sense, including all divine revelation.[8] Craigie took a somewhat similar view.[9] Kraus suggested that it refers primarily to the Pentateuch, though not in a 'nomistic' sense; but he also anticipated the view of other recent scholars whose work has been considered above, extending the meaning to include revelation in general but primarily the Psalter.[10] But this opinion is not unanimously held: the view that the reference is exclusively to the laws of the Pentateuch still has its representatives. B. Lindars, for example, in an article on Torah in Deuteronomy, argued that these psalms reflect Deuteronomic teaching in their use of Torah.[11] Several other scholars (notably Schmidt, but also more recently Kraus and Jacquet) have pointed to the significance of parallels with Deuteronomic or Deuteronomistic texts (Josh. 1.8; Deut. 17.18-19; 31.9-11). In sum, it must be concluded that Psalm 1 clearly refers to a written corpus which can be the subject of meditation, but that there is no evidence that this is the Psalter.

How, then, is Psalm 1 related to the rest of the Psalter? It cannot be said that this psalm in any way sums up the very diverse themes found in the book. The theme of the contrast between the respective fates of the wicked and the righteous (*ṣaddîqîm*) which is the main, and indeed the only, theme of Psalm 1 is certainly one that recurs frequently in the Psalms, but it is far from being their principal theme. In what sense, then, can this psalm be regarded as an introduction to the Psalter?

It is true that it is an admirably succinct statement of the character of the perfectly faithful, pious persons who will in due course have their reward. It describes the behaviour of such a person: he avoids the

8. M. Dahood, *Psalms 101–150* (AB, 17a; Garden City, NY: Doubleday, 1970), p. 173.

9. P.C. Craigie, *Psalms 1–50* (WBC, 19; Waco, TX: Word Books, 1983), p. 60.

10. H.-J. Kraus, *Psalmen I* (BKAT; Neukirchen–Vluyn: Neukirchener Verlag, 1961), pp. 4-5.

11. B. Lindars, 'Torah in Deuteronomy', in P.R. Ackroyd and Lindars (eds.), *Words and Meanings: Essays Presented to David Winton Thomas* (Cambridge: Cambridge University Press, 1968), pp. 117-36.

wicked and their ways and employs himself in reciting the Law of Moses day and night. It may thus be supposed that this person, who is now about to read the Psalms for his spiritual edification, will interpret them in the spirit of the teaching of the Law. In this sense the notion of 'hermeneutical spectacles' may be right: the pious individual nurtured in the teaching of the Pentateuch will certainly approach the Psalms in a spirit quite different from the spirit in which most of them were composed—a spirit which, it may be observed, is not essentially different from that in which more recent piety has approached them. Although they are not themselves Yahweh's Torah, they are rich sustenance for a Torah-oriented religious person. Psalm 1, and others of a similar nature scattered throughout the Psalter, do support the view that a new interpretation of the Psalms was being urged on the reader. It must be added, however, that this conclusion tells us nothing whatever about the *structure* of the Psalter.

It must, indeed, be acknowledged that the opinion, venerable as it is, that Psalm 1 was intended to function as an introduction to the Psalter is no more than an inference and is not susceptible of demonstration. Rather strangely the psalm has no superscription which might have stood, as in the case of some other Old Testament books (Deuteronomy, Nehemiah, Proverbs and several of the prophetical books) as a descriptive title either of this psalm, a group of psalms, or the whole Psalter. The opening word *ʾašrê*, 'Happy is...', is not an indication of the beginning of a book: it occurs 26 times in the Psalter, often but not invariably as the opening word of a single psalm. Several scholars have declared Psalm 1 to be 'not a true psalm', and doubts have been expressed about its poetical character. But if the final compilers of the Psalter intended that it should begin with the kind of statement that Psalm 1 makes, other psalms would seem to be equally appropriate; for example Ps. 19.8-15, or Psalm 119, which now sprawls incongruously between a psalm of thanksgiving and a lamentation, but which begins in a way similar to the first words of Psalm 1 and whose impassioned devotional spirit, expressed in terms of a personal testimony, might have served the purpose of introduction more appropriately. However this may be, the notion that the Psalter should have an introduction or 'preface' at all is not based on anything in the text: it is derived, in modern discussion at least, from a prior conviction that the Psalter must have a logical, or at least comprehensible, 'structure'.

The inclusion in the Psalter of certain psalms, notably the Torah psalms, may well point to a new mode of interpretation imposed on the whole collection. If this were so, however, such a reinterpretation could hardly have been achieved solely by the inclusion of a limited number of new, complete psalms. We should expect to find signs of reinterpretation *throughout* the Psalter. In many cases, undoubtedly, such reinterpretation will probably have left no traces in the text: it would have taken place silently in the mind of the reader. For example, Psalm 72, which is a prayer for the welfare of the king and for his dominion over the nations, was in all probability reinterpreted in eschatological terms as the expected future messianic king, but this reinterpretation could be carried out without textual tampering: indeed, in that instance the grandiose words about the king's world dominion were already hyperbolic and remote from reality even when the psalm was first composed, and the poetical language in which the psalm is couched would have made an eschatological interpretation an easy procedure. Many psalms may have been thus 'silently' reinterpreted without the necessity of any textual alteration. (See below on treatment of the 'royal' psalms.)

The only sure method by which it might be possible to pinpoint new interpretations of psalms is to look for additions or interpolations made to older psalms, or for examples of psalms that have been juxtaposed in order to suggest new meanings. Both of these methods admittedly involve, as do other methods, a considerable element of subjectivity, and they must be used with caution. They will be pursued in the following pages.

Interpolations of Torah Material

Psalm 19

This psalm offers a clear illustration of the reinterpretation of a psalm in terms of a different theology. The commentators are mainly agreed (Dahood is an exception) that its two parts, vv. 2-7 (known as 19A) and vv. 8-15 (19B), cannot have been composed by a single author. Psalm 19A, commonly classified as a hymn—or possibly a fragment of a hymn—speaks of the heavens specified as firmament, days and nights, and the sun, all of which God has created, as testifying silently to his glory. Psalm 19B, which begins abruptly with the announcement of a new subject, 'The Law of Yahweh', is a poem in praise of the Torah (for which a number of synonyms are employed, as in Ps. 119); it ends (vv. 12-15) with a prayer that the psalmist may be absolved from his previous failure to observe the Law and so may find acceptance by Yahweh and receive the great reward that is reserved for those who keep it. In addition to the apparent lack of connection between their themes, Psalms 19A and 19B differ radically in other ways: style, metre, genre, mood and even the use of divine names: 19A speaks of El, while 19B speaks of Yahweh.

While the older commentators Duhm and Gunkel regarded the two parts of the psalm as quite unrelated to one another (Duhm simply commented that Ps. 19B 'has not the slightest connection' with Ps. 19A either in form or content), most have recognized that their present combination cannot be accidental and that it calls for an explanation. The explanations offered differ considerably. Briggs suggested that the two originally separate poems may have been combined in order to make the point that 'the glory of Yahweh in the Law transcends His glory in the heavens'—implying theological correction or improvement of what was regarded as an inadequate prior statement. Schmidt also spoke of a theological development, but one which was by no means an improvement. Psalm 19B reflects a narrow view compared with the breadth of Psalm 19A. The glory of God is perceived in the psalm in two different ways; but the second way reflects a marked deterioration of religious thought from that of the first. Schmidt clearly held to the Wellhausian view that the religion of the post-exilic period with its concentration on the Law was inferior to that of the previous age.

Weiser found it difficult to determine the reason for the combination of the two parts; but he opined that the use of priestly language in v. 15 (*l*^{e}*rāṣôn*...*l*^{e}*pān*^{e}*kā*, 'to be acceptable in your presence' [cf. Lev. 1.3-4], though *rāṣôn* is as much a wisdom term as a priestly one), intended to affirm the efficacy of prayer and meditation rather than sacrifice, shows that the only link between the two original psalms was that both were used in public worship, of which they reflect different views. Kraus also saw a cultic connection between the two parts; he found hymnic elements in both. He too noted the presence of priestly language in Psalm 19B (*tāmîm* in v. 8), and also saw a link in vv. 12-15 with the 'Torah liturgy' of Psalm 15 with its enumeration of the qualities required of persons who desire to enter the temple, and a link between the 'speech' of the heavens in vv. 2-5 and the prayer for the acceptance of the psalmist's words in v. 15. He suggested that the purpose of the addition of Psalm 19B to 19A was to 'decode' the inaudible song of the heavens which cannot by itself reveal God. 'The cosmos celebrates God, but it does not teach his will.' Only the Law teaches who God is. It does what nature cannot do: it breaks through the sphere of guilt and restores the despairing.

Some later commentators have pointed out statements about the Law in Psalm 19B that appear by implication to compare the benefits conferred by the Law with those supplied by the sun, so making a strong link between the two halves of the psalm. Dahood suggested a number of emendations of the text and also of new interpretations of particular words in vv. 9-12. Thus *bārâʾ* in v. 9 means not 'pure' but 'radiant' (cf. Song 6.10), having its parallel in *m*^e*ʾîrat ʿênayim*, 'enlightening the eyes', in the same verse. In v. 12 *nizhār* is derived not from *zhr* II, 'warn', but from *zhr* I, 'shine'—so meaning 'enlightened'. These new renderings, if accepted, would strengthen the idea of the enlightenment of the eyes by the Law, and make plausible a connection with the immediately preceding verses about the sun (vv. 5b-7). The sun, providing the world with light, would then function as a kind of paradigm for the Law, the source of all 'enlightenment'.

Anderson agreed with Dahood about the meaning of *bārâ* in v. 9, and also pointed out other passages (Prov. 6.23; Ps. 119.105, 130) in which the Law is compared to a light or lamp. He further suggested that the relationship in ancient Near Eastern thought between the sun (Heb. *šemeš*) and justice (for example, the Babylonian sun-god Shamash presided over the administration of justice and dictated the Laws of Hammurabi to the king) may have been partly responsible for the juxtaposition of the solar imagery of Ps. 19.5b-7 with the imagery of light used of the Law in vv. 8-10. The author of Psalm 19B may have used the older poem as an introduction to his work. The whole poem speaks of the proclamation of God's glory; but 'whatever we can learn from nature cannot be compared to the law of the Lord'. Jacquet, while affirming that the two halves of the psalm have separate origins, found the movement from contemplation of the world to contemplation of the Torah a natural and logical one. Both nature and the Law call for a concert of praise. Jacquet suggested that the psalm in its final form was intended to be used both liturgically and as an expression of private piety.

O.H. Steck devoted an article to a critical consideration of Psalm 19.[12]

12. O.H. Steck, 'Bemerkungen zur thematischen Einheit von Psalm 19, 2-7', in R. Albertz *et al.* (eds.), *Werden und Wirken des Alten Testaments: Festschrift für Claus Westermann zum 70. Geburtstag* (Göttingen: Vandenhoeck & Ruprecht; Neukirchen–Vluyn: Neukirchener Verlag, 1980), pp. 318-24.

In addition to recognizing Psalms 19A and 19B as originally separate compositions, he also questioned the internal unity of 19A, for reasons that do not concern the present study. His main contribution to the solution of the question of the relationship between the two halves of the psalm was his observation that the praise of God's work in the creation of the universe in vv. 2-5a is expressed in the language of the wisdom teacher. The verbs *spr* (*piel*), 'recount' (v. 2) and *nbᶜ* (*hiphil*), 'pour forth' (v. 3), and the nouns *millâ*, 'word' (v. 5) and *daᶜat*, 'knowledge' (v. 3) are particularly characteristic of the wisdom literature, some of them almost exclusively so. Steck gave as examples passages from Job (11.6; 12.8-9; 13.17; 15.17; 32.6-11; 36.2-3; 38.4, 18) and Proverbs (15.2; 23.9), and also Ps. 78.2-4. So the silent 'message' that is proclaimed by and goes out into the world from heaven, day and night, about God's glory is a 'wisdom event' which Steck, following von Rad,[13] categorized as the 'self-revelation of creation' found in the book of Job and in the wisdom poems of Proverbs 1–9, through which God addresses human beings. It should be noted that if the hymnlike poem Psalm 19A is in fact the sophisticated product of a wisdom theology similar to that of Job rather than, as some commentators have supposed, an ancient Canaanite hymn to El, it may be by no means far removed in date from the praise of the Torah proclaimed in the second half of the psalm, though the Torah theology is not the same as that of the book of Job.

The most recent commentator on Psalm 19, Craigie, agreed with Steck that the psalm in its present form is a wisdom hymn. It is 'a subtle elaboration of Gen. 1–3, beginning with creation and its praise of God, but moving to something greater, the Torah of God and its place in the life of mankind'. It may be a single piece of writing, but it could also be seen as an old hymn complemented with a theological commentary. There is a close connection between the illumination and radiance of the life-giving sun and the divine Law that enlightens the eyes and illumines the servant of God. The contemplation of the sun shocks the readers into an awareness of their unworthiness (vv. 12-14). If the heavens extol God's glory, the readers pray that their own lives may be acceptable to God. Craigie saw v. 7b, 'there is nothing hidden from its heat', as the turning point of the psalm. Both sun and Torah dominate human life, but each is both welcome and terrifying, both life-imparting and also scorching and purifying. Both are essential to life. The final verse ties the

13. Von Rad, *Weisheit in Israel*, pp. 211ff.; ET *Wisdom in Israel*, pp. 160ff.

two themes together: 'the final words, describing the psalmist's relationship to God, transform God's universal and cosmic glory, with which the psalm began, into the glory of an intimate relationship between a human being and God, who offers solidarity and redemption'. The reference to the psalmist's words in v. 15 balances the statement about the 'speech' of the created world at the beginning of the psalm.

The foregoing survey of the commentaries shows that there has been a growing consensus of opinion that despite important differences between the two halves of Psalm 19 there are also close connections between them. The combination in a single psalm of the topics of the silent praise of God by his created works and of the praise of the Torah no longer seems as incongruous as it did to some earlier commentators. There is a general agreement that Psalm 19B is in some sense a theological commentary on Psalm 19A in which the thought of the Torah has moved to occupy the central place and now forms the climax of the whole. However, the majority of commentators still agree that the author of Psalm 19B was not the same as the author of Psalm 19A; two poems have been combined.

There are, however, still important areas of disagreement. There is no consensus whether Psalm 19A is an ancient cultic hymn or a (presumably later) wisdom psalm. Further, there are two different opinions about the composition of Psalm 19B; that is, on the question whether Psalm 19 is the result of the combination of two originally quite separate psalms (which must presumably presuppose that the synthesizer was fortunate, or especially inspired, to find two such psalms which by chance illuminated one another in this way), or whether Psalm 19B was deliberately composed and appended to an older Psalm 19A by a writer who had a theological comment to make on it. Given the undoubted affinities between the two halves that have been pointed out by recent commentators, the latter is by far the more satisfactory solution to the problem. Psalm 19 should therefore be understood as an example of a post-exilic addition made to an already existing psalm, expressing a Torah-oriented theology of which there is no hint in the original psalm. Whether with this addition the psalm was intended for some kind of (non-sacrificial liturgical?) use or was composed and placed in the Psalter for devotional or instructional use for individual readers cannot be determined from the text; clearly, however, it expresses the thoughts of an individual whose life centred on the Torah and its observance. There is no apparent meaningful relationship to the psalms that immediately precede and follow it that might provide a clue to the purpose of the arrangement of the Psalms in the Psalter, or at least this part of it.

Apart from the two psalms in which the Torah is the central theme throughout (Pss. 1 and 119) there are, then, others which in their present form teach that observance of the Torah is the central requirement of faith, but in which this teaching appears to be a secondary addition.

Psalm 37

Strictly speaking one cannot speak of 'interpolations' with regard to this psalm, as it has the form of an alphabetic acrostic; that is, it is a collection of originally independent sayings formed on the alphabetic principle. It is therefore correct to say that the sole reference to the Torah (vv. 30-31) is an originally independent saying which has no literary 'context'. It has, however, a theological or ideological context, in that the whole psalm is a didactic poem which asserts the truth of the principle of retribution (see for example vv. 25-26, 35-36) against the pretensions of the wicked, who perform their evil deeds in defiance of this principle (cf. Brueggemann, who interprets the psalm in a new and intriguing way [14]). Verses 30-31, which speak of the righteous who have the Torah in their hearts and are thus protected from disaster, and who also meditate (*hāgâ*; cf. Ps. 1.2) wisdom (*ḥokmâ*) and speak justice (*mišpāṭ*), are in general agreement with the rest of the psalm, but by their use of the word *tôrâ* they adopt a slightly different theological stance from the wisdom theology of the other sayings in the poem.

Psalm 40

In Psalm 40, as in Psalm 37, there is only one reference to the Torah (v. 9), in a verse that corresponds closely to both Ps. 1.2 and Ps. 37.31, with the phrases 'I delight to do your will' and 'Your law is within my heart' (*mēʿāy*, literally 'my entrails'), signifying a wholehearted devotion to the Torah. This verse occurs in the first part of the psalm (vv. 2-13), which has the form of an individual thanksgiving for deliverance from trouble (vv. 14-18, which are identical with Ps. 70, may have originally been a separate psalm, though some scholars—Weiser, Ridderbos,[15] Craigie—have argued for the unity of the whole psalm [vv. 2-18]). The text of vv. 7-8 is not entirely certain; apart from other problems, it is

14. W. Brueggemann, *The Psalms and the Life of Faith* (Minneapolis: Fortress Press, 1995), pp. 235-57.

15. N.H. Ridderbos, 'The Structure of Psalm xl', *OTS* 14 (1965), pp. 296-304.

disputed whether the 'scroll of the book' in v. 8 refers to the Torah. Most commentators regard v. 9 as integral to the psalm, although Kraus remarked that the reference to the Torah here introduces an entirely new note. Verse 9 is no doubt to be understood especially in conjunction with v. 7, which states that Yahweh does not require animal sacrifices but that he has given the psalmist 'an open ear', presumably to listen to his Torah. It is not entirely certain that vv. 7-9 are an interpolation giving a new meaning to the psalmist's thanks for Yahweh's gracious deeds (v. 6) in terms of the gift of the Torah, but this is strongly suggested by the above-mentioned resemblance to verses in Psalms 1 and 37. A transition from the proclamation of Yahweh's deeds in v. 6 to 'telling the good news' in v. 10 without the intervention of vv. 7-9 would be a natural one and would conform to the structural pattern of individual psalms of thanksgiving.

Psalm 78

This is another psalm into which interpolations characteristic of Torah theology have been inserted, though here an interesting distinction comes to the fore in that this psalm is best understood as being itself a wisdom psalm. It is a survey of Israelite history up to the time of David, in which moral judgments are made that are redolent of Deuteronomic theology. Whether it was intended for recital in public worship is disputed (see the different views of Kraus, Dahood, Anderson, Jacquet and Carroll[16]). That the psalm is a didactic poem by a teacher of wisdom is especially clear from vv. 1-3, where language characteristic of the wisdom teacher is piled up, especially *ḥiṭṭâ ʾōzen*, 'incline the ear', v. 1 (cf. Prov. 4.20; 5.1, 13), *ʾimrê pî*, 'the words of my mouth', v. 1 (cf. Prov. 4.5; 5.7; 7.24; 8.8), *māšāl*, 'proverb', v. 2, *nbʿ* (*hiphil*), 'pour out (of words)', v. 2 (cf. Ps. 119.171; Prov. 1.23; 15.2, 28; this word occurs only in Psalms and the wisdom literature), *ḥîdâ*, 'riddle, obscure saying', v. 2 (cf. Prov. 1.6). The use of *tᵉbûnâ*, 'understanding, wisdom', in the final verse (v. 72), a word that occurs 19 times in Proverbs, is a further indication of wisdom style. The occurrence of *tôrâ* in v. 1, in the sense not of Yahweh's Torah but of the teaching of a human wisdom teacher, a sense in which it occurs frequently in Proverbs (1.8; 3.1; 4.2; 6.20; 7.2) is of particular interest: this is its invariable meaning in Proverbs, but it is quite inconsistent with the meaning of the only other occurrences

16. R.P. Carroll, 'Psalm lxxviii: Vestiges of a Tribal Polemic', *VT* 21 (1971), pp. 133-50.

of *tôrâ* in this psalm (vv. 5, 10), where it clearly signifies the Law. This is in itself an indication that vv. 5 and 10 are interpolations, since it would be unlikely that the same writer would use the word in two quite different senses in the same psalm.

Briggs questioned the unity of the psalm, identifying vv. 4-7a, 10-11, and also v. 56b (where we find the word *ʿēdâ* in the plural, literally 'his testimonies', a frequent synonym for the Law in Ps. 119) as 'legalistic glosses'. It is in vv. 5 and 10 (apart from v. 1), and only there, that the word *tôrâ* occurs. The text of vv. 5-7a has long been regarded with suspicion as being prosaic in form rather than poetical (cf. recently Jacquet). But in fact the whole of vv. 5-8 with its emphasis on the Torah stands out from the rest of the psalm as a thematic intrusion: while the psalm as a whole is concerned with recounting Yahweh's deeds in Egypt, in the exodus, in the wilderness and in the land of Canaan and with the people's rebellion and his forbearance, these verses interrupt the sequence with a reference to the giving of the Law and the need to keep it. This theme is continued into v. 10. That the difficult v. 9 with its reference to the Ephraimites is also an interpolation and probably also corrupt has been frequently suggested since Gunkel (see Kraus's note and also *BHS* margin). If this is correct, the 'they' of v. 10 refers to Israel as a whole and the verse is a continuation of vv. 5-8.

The reference to God's *ʿēdôt* in v. 56b may, as Briggs suggested, be a gloss. Briggs proposed, on the analogy of the similar verses 17-18 and 40-41, where the words 'tested' and 'rebelled' appear as a pair but in separate parallel lines, that v. 56a was originally a poetical couplet that was subsequently compressed into a single line to make room for the 'legalistic gloss' in v. 56b. These are the only references to the Law in Psalm 78: v. 37 refers rather to Israel's rejection of God's covenant (*bᵉrît*), which stands parallel to his Torah in v. 10 but not elsewhere in the psalm.

Finally, it may be remarked that the word *tôrâ* occurs only in nine psalms.[17]

17. Pss. 1.2; 19.8; 37.31; 40.9; 78.1, 5, 10; 89.31; 94.12; 105.45; 119 (*passim*, 25 times). Not all these are interpolations into these psalms. More numerous are interpolations and additions made to psalms in the interest of wisdom theology; these will be considered below.

Interpolations of Wisdom Material

Psalm 18

While some commentators (Weiser, Jacquet, Craigie) have regarded this psalm, which also recurs in a similar version as 2 Samuel 22, as a literary unity, others have demurred. Schmidt thought it to be a combination of two separate psalms (vv. 2-31, 32-51). Others (Gunkel and most recently Vesco[18]) argued that it is a composite work, made from a variety of different materials. It is ostensibly a royal (individual) psalm of thanksgiving for deliverance from enemies, and it is attributed in its superscription and by its position in 2 Samuel to David. Again, there is no agreement among the commentators: some have held it to be very ancient, deriving from a period not far removed from the time of David, while others have considered it to be an expression of a post-exilic glorification of David, possibly with eschatological, messianic overtones.

Verses 21-28 have been singled out by several scholars as alien to their context. Briggs regarded vv. 21-24 as a 'legal gloss'. Gunkel held that the poem contains very varied material, and remarked on the 'colourlessness' of vv. 21-25 in contrast with the vivid description of Yahweh's theophany in vv. 8-16 and of his action in assisting David in war in vv. 33-37. Kraus pointed out similarities of vocabulary in vv. 21-28 with the terminology of Psalms 1 and 19. The most radical analysis of the composition of the psalm as a whole was carried out by Vesco, who regarded it as a late work of 'midrashic exegesis' on the life of David, in which the psalmist had gathered together and reinterpreted this material in order to present David as a model for the worshippers of his own time. Vesco detected Deuteronomic themes in vv. 21-28.

In fact an examination of the vocabulary employed in vv. 21-28 shows that these verses are not notably characterized by Torah theology as reflected in Psalms 1 and 19 or by Deuteronomic theology. *Mišpāṭîm* and *ḥuqqôt* (v. 23), for example are not words confined to Deuteronomy, while *mišpāṭ*, though it occurs in this sense in Psalms 1 and 19, is also found elsewhere. A wisdom affinity is in fact equally plausible: for example, *šāmar derek*, 'to keep the way', is a phrase that occurs several times in Proverbs. The precise character of these verses and their relationship or contrast with other parts of the psalm are more to the point.

This is the only passage in Psalm 18 in which 'David' speaks of his

18. J.-L. Vesco, 'Le psaume 18, lecture davidique', *RB* 94 (1987), pp. 5-62.

own virtues, claiming to be pure and innocent, and in which he attributes Yahweh's protection of him from his enemies to his own moral character (v. 25). This claim of innocence is presented in rather general terms: clean hands, obedience to Yahweh's ways, and so on. Gunkel noted that this protestation of innocence is an exceptional element in an individual psalm of thanksgiving,[19] a genre in which the attitude of the psalmist is, almost without exception, humble rather than self-justificatory: this is the only example of the *Gattung* in which this motif is pursued *in extenso*. These verses (21-25) also stand out from the rest of the psalm by their introduction of introspection into a poem in which the entire accent is on God as the active agent. Although they cannot be specifically characterized as sapiential or Torah-oriented, they should be seen as an attempt to reinterpret a psalm that was already concerned to teach contemporaries the lesson that Yahweh faithfully protects those who 'take refuge' in him (v. 3), by a writer who wished to 'gild the lily' by presenting David not only as faithful to Yahweh but also as morally perfect.

Psalm 27

The majority of commentators have considered this psalm to be the result of the combination of two originally independent psalms (vv. 1-6, 7-14). The main reason for this judgment is that the sequence of a psalm of confidence followed by a lamentation is difficult to account for. Kraus, Schmidt and Craigie nevertheless attempted to envisage a scenario for the whole psalm. However, the psalmist in the second part, at least in v. 11, speaks a different language from that employed in the first part of the psalm. The case for the majority opinion is therefore an attractive one: that is, that vv. 7-14 are the work of a different and later writer.

Verse 11 contains textual difficulties and is perhaps incomplete; but the key phrase, *hôrēnî yhwh dark^{e}kā*, 'Teach me, O Yahweh, your way', is significant. The notion of God as teacher, without intermediaries, of a human being is rare in the Old Testament. The verb *hôrâ* is most frequently used of human teachers, and especially of the priests; but its use here is patently derived from the wisdom literature, where it is used of a human teacher of wisdom (see for example Prov. 4.4, 11). In addition, it occurs with God as subject in only four psalms apart from Psalm 27: Pss. 25.8, 12; 32.8; 86.11; 119.33, 102. These psalms are all either

19. *Einleitung in die Psalmen*, p. 271.

wisdom or Torah psalms or psalms into which wisdom teaching has been interpolated. Ps. 27.7-14 as a whole may therefore be a wisdom passage that has been subsequently added to vv. 1-6; or, alternatively, v. 11 alone could be a wisdom interpolation. The latter alternative is the more probable, as the reference to Yahweh as teacher has no direct relationship to its context and could be omitted from its surroundings without disturbing the flow of the discourse, and also because the psalmist's desire to 'see the face' of Yahweh in v. 8 probably refers to a desire to enter the temple, which, though not incompatible with the desire for divine instruction, is not otherwise a feature of wisdom theology. If that is correct, we have here a reinterpretation of an older psalm in wisdom terms.

Psalm 32

Some commentators (Gunkel, Weiser, Anderson; cf. also Mowinckel[20] and Murphy[21]) have held this psalm in its entirety to be a wisdom psalm. Others (Briggs, Kraus, Jacquet, Craigie) considered that a wisdom section has been added to an older psalm of thanksgiving. Kraus in particular drew attention to the change of metre that occurs at v. 8. (The view of several scholars that vv. 1-2 also manifest wisdom features is erroneous: the term *ʾašrê*, 'Happy is [are]...', with which the psalm begins admittedly occurs in wisdom and Torah psalms, but is by no means exclusively characteristic of such psalms; and there are no other specifically wisdom terms in these verses.)

Verses 8-9, on the other hand, have all the characteristics of the wisdom instruction. The speaker here addresses an inexperienced person in general terms in the character of a wisdom teacher addressing a pupil, giving instruction on how to live. In v. 8 the verbs *hiśkîl* and *hôrâ*, both with the sense of 'teach, instruct', are used by the teacher (for the former word see Prov. 1–9 *passim* and also Prov. 16.23, and for the latter Ps. 27.11), as is 'to walk in the way' (cf. Prov. 1.15; 2.13, 20; 3.23); further, the teacher also undertakes to 'keep his eye' on the pupil. In v. 9 he uses an animal illustration to support his advice to the pupil (cf. Prov. 6.6-8; 30.24-31): horse and mule are without understanding (*ʾên hābîn*—another characteristically wisdom term).

The identity of the speaker here is disputed: is the 'I' of v. 8 the same as the 'I' of the rest of the psalm? If not, these verses may be a

20. 'Psalms and Wisdom', p. 213.

21. 'A Consideration', pp. 161-62.

(somewhat unexpected and incongruous) interpolation into the psalm by a wisdom teacher, drawing a lesson from the original thanksgiving psalm, pointing out the folly of sinners (v. 5) but adding a warning that in order to be a faithful worshipper (*ḥāsîd*, v. 6) it is necessary not only to pray to God but also to be properly instructed in behaviour acceptable to him. Alternatively, the speaker of these verses may be Yahweh himself: divine oracles, or the citation of them, occur fairly frequently in the Psalter (see for example Ps. 91.14-16), though they are not elsewhere expressed in such a formally didactic fashion.

A third possibility would be that vv. 8-9 are the words of the original psalmist, drawing these lessons from his own experience as recounted in vv. 3-5. In fact he begins to do this in v. 6 when he urges others to pray to God when in distress. But the earlier part of the psalm contains no reference to the psalmist's *ignorance*—only to his sin and folly. The teaching of vv. 8-9 is specifically about *learning* how to behave; this does not follow logically from the earlier verses, although it may have been the fact that the psalmist gives advice to others (as in other individual psalms of thanksgiving) that suggested to the author of vv. 8-9 the interpolation of further advice.

The main psalm is principally about sin, confession and forgiveness. Whether or not this forgiveness was understood as the result of an act of cultic sacrifice with a following blessing pronounced by a priest (there is no agreement among the commentators on this point), there is no mention of sin and forgiveness in vv. 8-9—only of accepting the true teaching. It may also be remarked that the thread of the discourse is in no way affected by the omission of vv. 8-9, which is therefore best understood as a didactic interpolation expressed in wisdom terminology and imagery.

Psalm 86

This psalm, which begins and ends with individual lamentation but has an individual thanksgiving at its centre, was called by Duhm 'a collection of quotations'. Kraus also noted that several verses or parts of verses are taken from other psalms, but saw this psalm as a late composition incorporating various traditional elements. Verse 11a is identical with Ps. 27.11a, which has been identified above as part of a wisdom interpolation. Several commentators see the phrase *hôrēnî yhwh dark^{e}kā*, 'Teach me thy way, O Yahweh', here as referring to the Law. There is little doubt that v. 11 is an isolated interpolation inserted between the hymnic

vv. 8-10 and the thanksgiving of vv. 12-13 with the purpose of adding a prayer for instruction to a section that is concerned with the praise of Yahweh for his greatness and salvific action. Other verses have been identified as having close affinities with the wisdom Psalm 25 (on which see below).

Psalm 92

There can be no doubt that vv. 7-8 of this psalm belong to the wisdom tradition. The phrase *ʾîš baʿar*, 'stupid man', in v. 7 occurs nowhere else in the Old Testament, but the word *baʿar* itself, which occurs also in the wisdom psalm 73 (v. 22), is found elsewhere only in Proverbs (12.1; 30.2). In the same verse *k*ᵉ*sîl*, 'fool', is also exclusively a wisdom word: it occurs 45 times in Proverbs and 17 times in Ecclesiastes; elsewhere in the Psalms twice: 49.11 and 94.8. *yādaʿ*, 'to know', occurs frequently in Proverbs in discussions about the wise and foolish; *bîn*, 'to understand', occurs 13 times in Job and 12 times in Proverbs, in addition to 12 occurrences in the *hiphil* in the sense of 'teach, instruct'. It also occurs seven times in Psalm 119.

Also characteristic of the wisdom literature is the implied identification in vv. 7-8 of the fool with the wicked. The verb *prḥ*, 'to flourish', also occurs in Prov. 11.28 and 14.11 with reference to the respective fates of the righteous and the wicked. If vv. 7-8 are in fact an insertion into the psalm, it may be possible to account for their insertion at this point: they may have been intended to follow up the thought of v. 6b, in which it is stated that Yahweh's thoughts (*maḥšābôt*) are very deep (*m*ᵉʾ*ōd ʿām*ᵉ*qû*). Originally this statement, in view of v. 6a, which praises Yahweh for the greatness of his deeds (*maʿ*ᵃ*śm*), was not a statement about his wisdom. But it is unique in its expression; and if the interpolator understood it in such a sense (cf. Akkadian *emēqû*, 'to be wise'), he may have judged it appropriate to add that those who have not accepted the gift of wisdom that he offers are to be accounted among the wicked.

There are also strong wisdom (or Torah) overtones in vv. 13-15. The verb *prḥ*, 'flourish', is used again (vv. 13, 15) with reference to the righteous. Further, their flourishing *like a palm tree* (v. 13) is close to the statement in Ps. 1.3 that those who delight in the Law are like trees that will prosper and not wither. It is to be noted that the rare word *šātûl*, 'planted', is also used in Ps. 1.3, where the righteous are compared with trees planted by the water.

Most commentators have regarded Psalm 92 as a literary unity with wisdom features. It is basically a psalm of praise of Yahweh coupled with thanks for his gracious actions couched in the form of a prayer by an individual ('I', vv. 5, 11, 12, 16), yet there are also clear references to community worship: the morning and evening sacrifices (v. 3), musical accompaniment (v. 4), the 'house of Yahweh' and its courts, in which the righteous are 'planted' (v. 14). Verses 6-10 and 13-15, however, are neither individual nor communal: they are impersonal statements of a general nature about the fates of righteous and wicked, wise and fools, in the manner of the book of Proverbs. There is therefore good reason to see this psalm as a liturgical composition that has been later interspersed with fragments of wisdom teaching.

Psalm 94

The redactional history of this psalm has affinities with that of Psalm 92, but the wisdom interpolation is more didactic in tone. Both the psalm's compositional unity and its present structure are disputed. Gunkel spoke of a 'mixed style'. He considered that it is basically a lamentation, vv. 1-7 being collective and vv. 16-23 individual. Verses 8-11 are a 'sermon' on the absurdity of the attitude of fools which takes its cue from v. 7. Verses 12-13 also are characteristic of wisdom literature. Other commentators (Schmidt, Weiser, Anderson, Jacquet) distinguished two sections, vv. 1-11 and 12-23; Schmidt held that these two parts are so different from one another that they must originally have been two quite distinct psalms. Kraus distinguished four sections: vv. 1-7, 8-11, 12-15, 16-23.

The terminology and the thought of vv. 8-15 are indisputably those of wisdom. The tone of vv. 8-11 is entirely didactic. Verse 8 is an appeal to the dullards (*bōᶜᵃrîm*, cf. *ba'ar* in Ps. 92.7) to understand (*bîn*, cf. again Ps. 92.7) and to the fools (*kᵉsîlîm*) to be wise (*hiśkîl*, cf. Ps. 119.99). The argument in v. 9 that since Yahweh created ear and eye he must himself be able to hear and see (denied by the wicked in v. 7) is the same as that used in Prov. 20.12. This verse also employs the word *hibbîṭ*, 'see, look' (cf. Ps. 119.6, 15, 18). In v. 10 Yahweh appears as the teacher of humanity: he disciplines the nations (*hôkîaḥ*, a frequent word in Job and Proverbs) and teaches knowledge to humankind (*hamᵉlammēd ʾādām daᶜat*, cf. again Ps. 119, nine times). The assertion in v. 11 that Yahweh knows (*yādaᶜ*) that the thoughts of human beings are *hebel*—vanity or emptiness—is reminiscent of Ecclesiastes, where this word is the leading motif of the book.

But this teaching is expressed with somewhat different nuances in vv. 8-11 and 12-13 respectively: while vv. 8-11 are statements *about* Yahweh in the style of the wisdom teacher and addressed to the 'fools', the form of vv. 12-13 is that of a prayer *to* him. To this extent those commentators who postulated a break between vv. 1-11 and 12-23 were correct, but not to the extent that the whole psalm should be divided into two sections, vv. 1-11 and 12-23. Verses 8-11 and 12-13 are closely related to one another. Verses 12-13, introduced by the word *ʾašrê*, certainly read like a new beginning; but this is probably to be explained as showing that vv. 12-13 are a *secondary* interpolation following the first in vv. 8-11. They introduce a reinterpretation of vv. 8-11 in that they speak of the Torah: Yahweh teaches those who accept his instruction 'out of your Torah' (*mittôrātᵉkā*, v. 12). But the whole of this section, vv. 8-15, speaks a different language from that of the rest of the psalm.

Psalm 105

This psalm is perhaps a doubtful case. The final verse (v. 45) undeniably speaks the language of the Deuteronomists and of the Torah theology. The keeping of Yahweh's statutes (*šāmar ḥuqqâw*) occurs frequently in Deuteronomy and also in Kings; the keeping of Yahweh's law (*nāṣar tôrôt*) is also mentioned in Ps. 119.34 (where however *tôrâ* is in the singular), and *nāṣar* with objects synonymous with *tôrâ* (*ʿēdôt*, *ḥuqqôt*, *piqqûdîm*, *miṣwôt*) occurs frequently in that psalm. The conjunction *baʿᵃbûr*, if it means 'in order that' here, implies that obedience to Yahweh's laws is the sole object of Yahweh's action in bringing Israel out of Egypt and giving the lands of the nations into their possession—a Torah-centred theology equalled only in such psalms as 1 and 119. In the rest of the psalm there is no mention of Yahweh's Law as an obligation imposed on Israel—only a reference to the covenant (*bᵉrît*) and oath (*šᵉbûʿâ*) which he made as a promise to the patriarchs and which he confirmed as a 'statute' (*ḥōq*, vv. 8-9). On the other hand it could be argued—though it is generally regarded as a cultic poem—that the whole psalm has a didactic character. Nevertheless the reference to the Torah in v. 45 is unexpected, and suggests that that verse (or vv. 44-45) may be a later addition (see below on Ps. 107).

Psalm 107

The final verse of this psalm (v. 43) is undoubtedly the word of a wisdom teacher whose intention was to urge his readers to take the previous verses as instruction in wisdom. That it is an appendix, or part of an appendix, to the psalm is made quite certain by the fact that v. 43a is verbally identical with Hos. 14.10a. It is universally recognized that Hos. 14.10 is an appendage to the book of Hosea, to which it is otherwise unconnected, added by a wisdom teacher to perform the same function for the interpretation of a prophetical book as Ps. 107.43 performs for Psalm 107. Sacred Scripture, whether it is prophecy or psalmody, was to be interpreted in terms of wisdom theology. This understanding of the final verse of Psalm 107 tends to confirm the conclusion reached about the final verse of Psalm 105. The rest of Psalm 107—or at least vv. 1-32—was intended for cultic use rather than for private meditation.

Several commentators (see also Beyerlin[22]) noted that vv. 33-43 differ in various ways from vv. 1-32; in particular, that they lack the refrain that characterizes the latter (vv. 8-9, 15-16, 21-22, 31-32), and that they are of a more general character. Kraus described vv. 33-43 as a hymn, whereas vv. 1-32 are a psalm of thanksgiving. Beyerlin among others maintained that all these final verses—not only v. 43—are a paraenetic and didactic wisdom poem which teaches the doctrine of retribution. However this may be, there is a good case for seeing the whole of vv. 33-43 as different from the rest of the psalm; but v. 43, with its distinctive wisdom language (*ḥākām*, 'wise', *hitbônān* [*hithpolel* of *bîn*], 'consider'), stands by itself as a clear example of wisdom teaching which is absent from at least vv. 1-32.

Psalm 111

This psalm resembles Psalm 37 in that it is an alphabetic acrostic and that it has been composed as a collection of quotations of short pieces arranged alphabetically. It differs, however, in that here each letter of the alphabet is represented by a single line or stichos comprising only three or four words. Some of these lines hardly complete whole sentences by themselves. To have composed the psalm in this way involved great ingenuity, but precluded the development of any real sequence of thought (see especially Gunkel's comments). Dahood drew attention to the unusual word order in some lines, where the author (better, 'compiler') was forced to invert the usual order so as to produce lines that begin with the appropriate letters. There are didactic notes in v. 2, which asserts that

22. W. Beyerlin, *Werden und Wesen des 107. Psalms* (BZAW, 153; Berlin: de Gruyter, 1979).

Yahweh's great deeds are (to be) studied or reflected on (*dārûš*, cf. Ps. 119.45, 94, 155) by all that delight in them (*ḥepᵉṣêhem*, cf. Ps. 1.2; 119.35), and in v. 5 with its reference to 'those who fear him' (*lîrēʾēhâw*). The climax of the psalm occurs in v. 10, introduced by the standard wisdom motto, 'The fear of Yahweh is the beginning of wisdom' (*rēʾšît ḥokmâ yirʾat yhwh*), which is identical with Prov. 9.10 (cf. Prov. 1.7; Job 28.28) and which promises the acquisition of 'good sense' (*śēkel ṭôb*) by those who practise wisdom. The psalm as a whole, however, combines elements of a psalm of thanksgiving and a hymn, praising Yahweh for his great deeds and for the benefits conferred on his people; the lines that the compiler has borrowed and arranged to express this theme do not in general have a wisdom character in themselves. The compiler has attempted to put a wisdom stamp on the whole by commending the actions of Yahweh as a subject of reflection in v. 2 and by quoting the standard identification of the fear of Yahweh with wisdom in the final verse.

Psalm 144

It is generally recognized that this psalm is composite and that it makes use of a variety of traditional themes and literary styles. It is not easy to see what thematic development exists in or between its various parts: the psalmist's praise of Yahweh for giving him the strength of a successful conqueror in vv. 1-2, the general reflection on the ephemeral character of human nature in vv. 3-4, the hymn-like section vv. 9-10, followed by a request to be delivered from enemies in v. 11 and the prayer for material prosperity in vv. 12-15. The psalm was regarded by some commentators as a collection of unrelated fragments. Others have held that it is the result of the combination of two (Briggs, Gunkel, Dahood) or three (Duhm) quite unrelated psalms. Others have attempted to discern some kind of unity in the psalm, seeing it as a 'cultic liturgy' (Schmidt, Weiser, Anderson).

Verses 3-4 are expressed in quite impersonal terms and are a reflection on human nature (*ʾādām, ben-ʾᵉnôš*) in general. They combine an almost exact verbal echo of Ps. 8.5 (v. 3) with a variant of Ps. 39.6 (v. 4), using the terms 'breath' (*hebel*) and 'shadow' to describe human life. In both Psalms 8 and 39 the passages in question occur in appropriate contexts; here they do not. So incongruous are they in their present position that Duhm concluded that vv. 3-4 here must be an irrelevant interjection, a gloss transcribed by a pious reader into the margin of his copy of the Psalter expressing his own conviction about human nature and subsequently incorporated accidentally into the text of the psalm. Their theme is found elsewhere in the wisdom literature (see for example Ps. 90.3-10; 94.11 [*hebel* again]; Ecclesiastes *passim*).

Psalm 146

This psalm, like Psalm 144, appears to have been composed by the combination of motifs gathered from elsewhere (so Gunkel and Kraus). In form it is basically an individual hymn of praise in which Yahweh is extolled as creator and for his care for the oppressed. Verses 3-4, however, are in the form of a (plural) imperative; Kraus characterized them as a didactic address conveying an admonition. They speak first of the unreliability of help that might be expected from the powerful (*nᵉdîbîm*), but then extend this thought to cover human beings in general (*ben-ʾādām*, cf. Ps. 118.8-9). Verse 4 speaks of the inevitability of death, which entails the failure of all human projects (cf. Ps. 144.3-4). The contrast between this negative thought about human life and the positive affirmation about the help that is available from God in v. 5 provides a possible context for vv. 3-4, but the didactic tone of the latter suggests an interpolation by a wisdom teacher into a psalm of a quite different genre.

Conclusion

The above analysis has shown that interpolations or additions have been made to about 15 psalms in the Psalter in order to reinterpret their original character and purpose, giving them a new orientation in terms of a wisdom or Torah theology. Their distribution among the five Books of the Psalter is uneven: six occur in Book I (including all the Torah additions), one each in Books II and III, three in Book IV and four in Book V. Probably some others could have been included in the list on a broader interpretation of 'wisdom'. A large number of the psalms so designated are composite also in other respects. Among the many additions that have been made to them in the course of time there are some (not examined here) in which certain lines or verses point to a wisdom tendency in the broad sense.

No clues can be adduced from the survey so far about an intention on the part of a final redactor to arrange the Psalter, or even part of the Psalter, in a particular order: the evidence obtained reveals no pattern of additions, but rather suggests no more than an attempt—or, more probably, a series of unrelated attempts—made at different times and by different persons to make such changes to particular psalms as seemed to invite such reinterpretation. However, the evidence is not yet complete. It is necessary to take into account those psalms that may be characterized as *wholly* wisdom psalms or *wholly* Torah psalms, and the possibility of the existence of links between them and adjacent psalms that have been given wisdom or Torah reorientations—links that might indicate patterns of arrangement.

Pure Wisdom and Torah Psalms

The identification of Torah psalms presents no problem. If Psalm 19 is to be regarded as a psalm to which a Torah addition has been made rather than as a pure Torah psalm, the Psalter contains only two pure Torah psalms: 1 and 119. The identification of pure wisdom psalms is, as has already been remarked, a difficult question. The following psalms, however, will now be considered in that connection.

Psalm 8

This psalm is couched in the form of a hymn to Yahweh whose name is glorious (*ʾaddîr*) throughout the world. Verses 3-9, however, are a meditation wholly concerned with his human creatures. Steck suggested that the psalm may originally have been a wisdom poem that was subsequently turned into a hymn by the addition of the initial and final verses;[23] but there are indications that these verses are integrally related to the rest: the references both to heaven and earth in v. 2 are picked up in the verses that follow, especially in vv. 4-5, where a comparison and contrast are drawn between the two aspects of the creation, the heavens and human beings. This is, then, wholly a 'wisdom' psalm in that it reflects on human nature in its two aspects, human frailty and mortality on the one hand and, on the other, the high status that has been granted to human beings (v. 6) together with their dominion over all other created beings (vv. 7-9). There are affinities here with Genesis 1–3 and with Job. There is nothing that directly suggests the cult (unless the obscure v. 3a refers to cultic song, which is extremely doubtful), although Kraus could be right in surmising that a traditional cultic theme may be remotely reflected here. The psalm is best seen as a wisdom psalm which calls on the readers to give thanks and praise to the creator for

23. O.H. Steck, 'Beobachtungen zu Psalm 8', in *Wahrnehmungen Gottes im Alten Testament* (TBAT, 70; Munich: Chr. Kaiser Verlag, 1982), pp. 221-31.

having conferred such honour on his human creatures. Unlike the 'enthronement psalms' 93 and 95–99, Psalm 8 is universalistic in that it speaks of humanity in general without any allusion, direct or indirect, to Israel, its special status or its temple, or to other nations.

Psalms 14 and 53

These two psalms are mainly identical though there are some variants, notably in 14.5; 53.6 and in the use of the divine names. Apart from the final verse, which expresses hope for the restoration of Israel and looks like a later addition (14.7 = 53.7 makes a satisfactory ending) the psalms teem with expressions characteristic of the wisdom literature. *ᶜaśâ ṭôb*, 'do good', perhaps better, '*be* good', is used in 14.1 = 53.2 in an absolute sense (it is contrasted with *hšḥît*, 'be corrupt'); this is a rare usage but also occurs in Pss. 34.15; 37.3, 27 and in Eccl. 3.12; 7.20. *maśkîl*, 'wise' (14.2 = 53.3) is almost exclusive to Proverbs and Job.[24] *yādaᶜ* used absolutely in the sense of 'have knowledge' (14.4 = 53.5) is found mainly in Proverbs and Ecclesiastes (Prov. 17.27; Eccl. 9.11). *nābāl*, 'fool', a word with an extremely pejorative nuance (14.1 = 53.2), is less exclusively a wisdom term, occurring only three times in Proverbs; but see Bennett on *nābāl* and on *ᶜēṣâ*, which occurs in 14.6.[25] The psalm, which is not addressed to God, identifies folly with wickedness, as is frequently done in Proverbs. It reflects on the ubiquity of fools/wicked and their attacks on the poor (*ᶜānî*) and on 'my people', whose only refuge is in God (14.4, 5; 53.5, 6), expressing confidence that he will come to their rescue. It is thus a general reflection on human wickedness, lacking any specific references—the references to the poor are conventional rather than specific.

Psalm 25

This alphabetic psalm presents itself as an individual lament; but several commentators have doubted whether it was composed for liturgical use, though it may have been used for that purpose at a later time. Duhm held it to be a 'mosaic' put together from earlier fragments. Schmidt, pointing out its lack of connected thematic sequence due to the constriction imposed by its alphabetic form, saw the psalm as a purely scribal product composed 'at the desk'. Craigie took it to be a companion piece to

24. Prov. 10.5; 14.34; 15.24; 16.20; 17.2; 19.14; 21.12; Job 22.2.

25. R.A. Bennett, 'Wisdom Motifs in Psalm 14 = 53: *nābāl* and *ʾēṣāh*', *BASOR* 220 (Dec. 1975), pp. 15-21.

Psalm 1, putting the theme of that psalm into the context of prayer. Ruppert categorized it as literature to be read rather than recited.[26] It is generally agreed that wisdom themes are prominent, especially in vv. 4-5, 8-10 and 12-15. There are frequent repetitions in these verses, due presumably to the requirements of the alphabetic arrangement.

In vv. 4-5 the psalmist requests God to make his ways known to him (*yādaʿ* [*hiphil*], *derek*), to teach him (*limmad*) his paths (*ʾōraḥ*) and to direct his ways. In vv. 8-10 God is called 'good' (*ṭôb*); he instructs sinners in the way and leads the afflicted (or humble, *ʿānî*) and, once again, teaches them his 'way'. Verses 12-13 speak of those who fear God and assert that he will teach them so that they will 'abide in prosperity' and that their children will 'possess the land'. These are all words and expressions, and themes, characteristic of the didactic wisdom literature, especially Proverbs. But somewhat similar language occurs in other verses: 'affliction' (*ʿānî* and *ʿ*^{o}*nî*) in vv. 16 and 18, 'guard my life' (*šomrâ napšî*) in v. 20, 'preserve me' (*yiṣṣ*^{e}*rûnî*) in v. 21.

The psalm oscillates between appeals to God (vv. 1-3, 6-7, 11, 16-20), expressions of confidence (vv. 14-15) and wisdom passages. But these themes are not incongruous: they may be compared with other psalms of lamentation into which appropriate wisdom passages have been inserted; all are consonant with the initial expression of trust in v. 1. Although the alphabetic form has dictated these abrupt changes in this psalm, there is no reason to see it as a mosaic of unrelated fragments. Almost all the commentators have held the final verse (v. 22), which stands outside the alphabetical scheme, to be a later addition made perhaps for liturgical reasons, introducing the theme of the plight of the nation. The psalm should be regarded as an integral wisdom psalm in which the psalmist has adopted the form of an individual lament.

Psalm 34

This psalm resembles Psalm 25 in many ways: it too is an alphabetic acrostic, and follows a scheme that has similar imperfections, notably the lack of a verse beginning with the letter *waw*; the final verse, which stands outside the alphabetic sequence, begins with the same word as the final verse of Psalm 25 and speaks similarly of Yahweh's redemptive action. A further similarity to Psalm 25 is that this final verse has been widely adjudged by modern scholars (though not by all commentators)

26. L. Ruppert, 'Psalm 25 und die Grenze kultorientierter Psalmenexegese', *ZAW* 84 (1972), pp. 576-82.

to be a later, liturgical addition to the original non-liturgical psalm (a 'reverse' reinterpretation, as it were). Some scholars have suggested that the two psalms have a common author.

The second half of the psalm (vv. 12-22) is clearly a wisdom instruction and strongly resembles the instructions of Proverbs 1–9. The invitation by a human wisdom teacher to his 'sons' (*bānîm*) to heed (*šāmaᶜ*) his instruction (*limmad*) about the fear of Yahweh, together with the verses that follow it, could easily belong to Proverbs 1–9 (*passim*, and especially Prov. 4.1, where as here the address is to 'sons' in the plural). Other expressions characteristic of the wisdom literature include 'to see good' (v. 13; cf. Job 7.7), the injunction to guard one's tongue (v. 15), 'turn from evil' (*sûr mērāᶜ*), frequent in Proverbs; 'do/be good' (*ᶜāśâ rāᶜ*, v. 15). The emphasis on the contrasted fates of wicked and righteous in vv. 16-21 is a major theme of Proverbs. Two topics scattered throughout the psalm bind the whole poem together: the fear of Yahweh (vv. 8, 10, 12) and the idea of goodness (*ṭôb*, vv. 9, 11, 13, 15, referring both to Yahweh's nature and to his gifts to the righteous—a word found frequently in other wisdom or Torah psalms, notably Ps. 119). The psalm is presented as a psalm of thanksgiving, and may describe the actual experiences of the author; but the intention throughout is clearly didactic: to help others to learn from these experiences (cf. especially Prov. 4.1-6). The psalm may therefore be legitimately classified as a wisdom psalm.

Psalm 39

This psalm has not generally been classified as a wisdom psalm, although some commentators (Anderson, Craigie) have drawn attention to the presence of wisdom features in it. The form, which is somewhat unconventional, is nevertheless that of an individual lament. There are some textual difficulties, but the thought is reasonably clear. Apart from the general reference to the wicked (*rāšāᶜ*) in v. 2 we find almost none of the complaints usual in individual laments, whether of illness or persecution. This is, however, an intensely personal psalm. In some respects it has affinities with Psalms 37 and 73. The psalmist is preoccupied with the thought of the ephemeral nature of human life and its insignificance in God's sight (vv. 5-7, 12, 13, 14), not only in general but specifically in relation to his own case (vv. 5-6, 13-14). The thought is especially close to that of Ecclesiastes: human life is three times characterized as *hebel* (vv. 6, 7, 12); there are also affinities with passages in Job. Other words characteristic of the wisdom literature are frequent throughout the psalm: *šāmar derek*, 'to guard one's way' (v. 2; cf. Prov. 2.8; 16.17); *tôkaḥat*, 'reproof, chastisement' (v. 12)—a rare word almost exclusive to Proverbs, with two other occurrences in the Psalms, 38.15 and 73.14, and two in Job; *tôḥelet*, 'hope' (v. 8); this is a word that occurs only six times in the Old Testament, of which three are found in Proverbs and one in Job. Verses 2-4, which speak of the psalmist's experiences, serve as an introduction to the thought expressed in the psalmist's reported words in vv. 5ff. His personal request to God to inform him (*yādaᶜ* [*hiphil*]) about his 'end' so that he may fully realize how ephemeral his life is (v. 5) is, like the verses that follow, in fact a warning to others to live their lives with this thought in mind. This didactic character clearly classifies the psalm as a wisdom psalm.

Psalm 49

All the commentators recognize this psalm as a wisdom psalm, or, more properly, a wisdom *song* (v. 5b), and there can be no doubt that it is. Thematically it has close affinities with Psalms 37, 39 and 73 and with Job and Ecclesiastes. The psalmist begins (vv. 2-5) by announcing his intention to appeal (*šimᶜû*, 'hear, pay attention') and 'give ear' (*haʾᵃzînû*, v. 2) to a universal audience ('all peoples' of all ranks and economic status); to speak wisdom (*ḥokmâ*) and to meditate (the noun *hāgût*, 'meditation', is cognate with *hāgâ*, 'to meditate', used in Ps. 1.2 with regard to Yahweh's *tôrâ*, and in Ps. 37.30 with *ḥokmâ* as its object). 'Understanding' (*tᵉbûnâ*) is used with *ḥokmâ*, a word pair also found in Proverbs. The author is thus clearly a wisdom teacher, but has been a pupil: in v. 5 he states that what he has to say is the result of listening ('inclining his ear', *hiṭṭâ ʾōzen*, cf. Prov. 4.20; 5.1, 13) to a proverb (*māšāl*) and solving a riddle (*ḥîdâ*, cf. Prov. 1.6 in a somewhat similar introduction by the teacher to his teaching). In v. 11 he speaks, as in Proverbs, of the wise (*ḥᵃkāmîm*) and of fools (*kᵉsîl*, *baᶜar*).

The entire psalm is pure wisdom teaching, basically on a single theme: human mortality and death. Verses 7-10 and 17-20 stress the worthlessness of material possessions which must be left to others when death comes, and vv. 13 and 21 declare that in death we are no different from the animals. These are major themes in Ecclesiastes. Verse 16 has been taken as a statement that the psalmist, presumably together with those who follow his teaching, will escape the fate of others and enjoy life after death; but this may not be a correct interpretation of the verse.

A remarkable feature of this psalm is that the psalmist states that he will solve (or perhaps propound) his riddle to musical accompaniment (*ʾeptaḥ bekinnôr ḥîdātî*, literally 'I [will] open my riddle with a lyre', v. 5). This has been taken to mean that the psalm was actually sung by the psalmist; and this raises an important question with regard to the *Sitz im Leben* of the psalm (and, by implication, of other 'wisdom' psalms as well), suggesting to most commentators that it was intended for public performance rather than to be read privately or listened to by pupils. Singing and musical accompaniment may well have been a feature of cultic hymns of praise (cf., for instance, Ps. 89.2); but, as Gunkel and Dahood pointed out, this is the only example of a wisdom instruction either in the Psalter or elsewhere in which music or musical accompaniment is mentioned. The explanation is probably to be found in understanding the reference to music as connected with the psalmist's *inspiration* rather than his singing. The psalmist speaks of listening (v. 5a), perhaps to catch a reminiscene echo of earlier wisdom teaching with which he had been familiar in his youth, but more probably to a word from God, that is, a divine instruction which he is to hand on. He is, then, not referring to musical accompaniment to a song: he has referred in v. 4 to the fact that what he is about to speak (*dibbēr*—he says nothing about singing) is the result of an earlier inner meditation (*hāgût libbî*). It was at this stage that his meditation had been accompanied by music. Analogies have been found in 1 Sam. 10.5; 16.16; 2 Kgs 3.15; none of these incidents has anything to do with wisdom instruction, but it is interesting to observe that in none of those passages is there any mention of singing to musical accompaniment.

Psalm 73

This psalm has often been compared to Psalms 37 and 49; in theme and expression it has close affinities both with Job and Ecclesiastes. Several commentaries describe it as a wisdom psalm; those who are hesitant to do so have nevertheless admitted its didactic character. There is no adequate reason (with, for example, Gunkel and Tournay[27]) to doubt that it is a unified composition. It is not a prayer, and it mainly speaks of God in the third person, although in one passage God is apparently addressed. It takes the form of a narrative in which the psalmist describes his spiritual struggles, which were caused by his inability to understand

27. R.J. Tournay, 'Le Psaume lxxiii: relectures et interprétation', *RB* 92 (1985), pp. 187-99.

why the wicked were prosperous while he, who saw himself as innocent, constantly had to bear suffering. He goes on to tell how his doubts about God were allayed when he entered the 'sanctuary of God' (*miqd^{e}šê-ʾēl*, v. 17) and learned through revelation that God would in the end destroy the wicked. This realization had led to a renewed confidence in God which he now expresses in an affirmation that whatever might happen to him he cannot be separated from his intimate relationship with God (vv. 23-26).

The narrative is interspersed with passages in which the psalmist reflects on his situation both past and present: first on the apparent escape of the wicked from punishment (vv. 3-12) and then on his later realization of their fate (vv. 18-20), his own foolishness in having doubted God (vv. 21-22) and his new confident belief for himself and for all who remain close to God (vv. 23-28). The conclusion of the psalm is thus a strong affirmation of the doctrine of retribution together with a recognition, whether actually based on the psalmist's personal experience or not, of the danger of falling into the temptation to lose one's trust in God's faithfulness. That its intention is to teach and warn others is strongly indicated by the references to knowledge—that is, wisdom. The psalm may be a didactic example story rather than a personal narrative; in any case it has the marks of a wisdom poem.

The doubts attributed to the 'people' (v. 10), who are represented as observing and remarking on the prosperity of the wicked (perhaps reading *ʿām* rather than *ʿammô*, 'his people'), and on God's apparent attitude towards them are expressed in terms of God's knowledge rather than his justice: 'How can God know (*yādaʿ*)?'; 'is there knowledge (*daʿat*) in the Most High?' (v. 11); and in v. 16 the psalmist seeks to understand (*dēʿâ*) the reason for the prosperity of the wicked before it is divinely revealed to him (v. 17): 'then I perceived their end' (*ʾabînâ l^{e}ʾaḥ^{a}rîtām*; the verb is characteristic of Job and Proverbs, and the noun is used of the fate of the wicked especially in Proverbs). The word 'stupid' (*baʿar*, v. 22) occurs only five times in the Old Testament: twice in Proverbs and in two other verses in the Psalms: 49.11 and 92.7. These are examples of specifically wisdom vocabulary.

There are no references in the psalm to public worship unless the psalmist's statement in v. 17 that his awareness of the ultimate fate of the wicked came to him when he entered the *miqd^{e}šê-ʾēl* is to be so interpreted. The phrase is unique, and its meaning, together with that of the whole line, is obscure. Some scholars (notably Kraus and Anderson) have taken it to refer to a visit to the temple, where the psalmist may have experienced a theophany. But other explanations have been suggested: Duhm, Jacquet and Nielsen[28] thought that the phrase might mean 'divine mysteries'—that is, the psalmist was privately initiated into God's secret thoughts. Dahood suggested that it refers to heaven, an idea supposedly consonant with the psalmist's expectation of life after death (vv. 23-26)—one of the possible, though disputed, interpretations of those verses. In fact the cultic explanation is only one among several and perhaps the least probable; it is certainly not possible to base a cultic interpretation of the psalm on this disputed verse.

Psalm 90

The dominating theme of this psalm, which has the form of a communal lament, is the ephemeral nature of human life in contrast to the eternal nature of the creator God, who sets a limit to human life and in his anger sweeps his human creatures away into oblivion. As a lamentation it is expressed in very general terms: it lacks any reference to a particular complaint. Although some commentators (Duhm, Briggs, Gunkel, Barnes, Jacquet) have regarded it as composite, others (Kraus, Anderson, von Rad[29]) have maintained its essential unity. Opinions have also differed on the question of its classification as a wisdom psalm, though all admit that it has been influenced by wisdom ideas. Verse 12 in particular has this character, with its appeal to God to act as teacher (*hōdaᶜ*), so that 'we' (i.e. those whom the psalmist claims to represent) may 'enter into the heart [or, possibly, "gate"[30]] of wisdom' (*ḥokmâ*). But the wisdom affinities are more extensive than this. The whole section lamenting the frailty of human life (vv. 3-12), for example, expresses a major theme of Ecclesiastes which is also frequently found in Job, especially Job 14.5-12, where similar imagery is used: in both

28. E. Nielsen, 'Psalm 73: Scandinavian Contributions', in A.G. Auld (ed.), *Understanding Poets and Prophets: Essays in Honour of George Wishart Anderson* (JSOTSup, 152; Sheffield: JSOT Press, 1993), pp. 273-83.

29. G. von Rad, 'Der 90. Psalm', in *Gottes Wirken in Israel: Vorträge zum Alten Testament* (Neukirchen–Vluyn: Neukirchener Verlag, 1976), pp. 268-83.

30. 'Door' or 'gate' would make better sense (cf. Prov. 8.34). It is possible that *lᵉbab* here may mean not 'heart' but 'into the gate'. The word *bāb* for 'gate' does not occur elsewhere in the Old Testament, but is common in later Hebrew; see M. Jastrow, *Dictionary of Talmud Babli, Yerushalmi, Midrashic Literature and Targumim* (New York: Pardes Publishing House, 1950), I, p. 136.

cases (Ps. 90.5-6; Job. 14.7-10) the ephemeral nature of human beings is compared to that of plants.

Von Rad argued with great emphasis that Psalm 90 is a wisdom psalm. He maintained that it sounds a discordant note in the Psalter and in the Old Testament as a whole, expressing a wisdom theology but not a conventional one, as in Proverbs; rather, a negative, utterly pessimistic theology akin to that of Qoheleth. Whereas some scholars understood the psalm as expressing a positive hope at least in vv. 11-17, von Rad stressed its sombre character, describing it as sceptical and almost cynical. He pointed out that despite its outward form as lamentation it makes no mention of God's deeds in the past as offering grounds for hope in the future, but speaks only of God's eternal being and of his hostility towards humankind. If there is any comfort for humanity in its wretched situation it could only be based on a recognition of God's power as creator; but this is no real comfort, since God's will and his intentions are hidden from us. Von Rad concluded that Psalm 90 was not in any way related to the public cult, but is the expression of the personal, gloomy reflections of a wisdom teacher like Qoheleth. Whether or not von Rad's assessment is correct, he has convincingly demonstrated the close affinity between the two texts and so substantiated the claim that this psalm should be classified as a pure wisdom psalm.

Psalm 112

This psalm, as all the commentators have observed, is very closely related to Psalm 111—so closely that it has been suggested that they have a common author. Psalm 111, as has been pointed out, contains wisdom elements but is not a pure wisdom psalm. Unlike Psalm 111, Psalm 112, though also an alphabetic acrostic, is not a collection of fragments but is much more structured and has a single theme: apart from the initial hallelujah ('Praise Yahweh'), which is not an integral part of the psalm itself, it is entirely concerned with the happiness of those who fear Yahweh and delight in his commandments (v. 1), also described as the 'upright' (*y^{e}šārîm*, vv. 2, 4), setting out their virtues and their reward, with a final verse which speaks by contrast about the jealousy and the final fate of the wicked (v. 10).

The similarities with Psalm 111 even extend, and in detail, to the poetical form. Both psalms are alphabetic acrostics in which each line—rather than, as is more usual, each couplet or verse—begins with the appropriate successive letter; and each ends with a three-line rather than a two-line verse to complete the alphabet. There are also remarkable similarities of vocabulary between the two psalms, though the words that they share are employed in different ways. Thus in Ps. 112.1 those who *fear* God delight (*ḥāpēṣ*) in his commandments, whereas in Ps. 111.2 the upright are engaged in *praising* him. In Ps. 112.6 the *righteous* will be remembered (*zēker*) for ever, but in Ps. 111.5 it is *Yahweh* who 'remembers' his covenant. Again in Ps. 112.8 it is the hearts of the upright that are said to be firmly established (*sāmûk*), while in Ps. 111.8 it is Yahweh's precepts (*piqqûdîm*) of which this is said. In Ps. 112.4 it is the righteous who are gracious and merciful (*ḥannûn wᵉrāḥûm*), whereas in Ps. 111.4 it is Yahweh to whom these characteristics are attributed. In Ps. 112.3 it is the upright whose righteousness endures for ever, but in Ps. 111.3 this phrase is used about Yahweh.

There is thus a curious transference of epithets between Yahweh on the one hand and those who obey him on the other. This suggests that one of these two psalms has been deliberately based on the other but with the intention of shifting the emphasis. It is more probable that it is the author of Psalm 112 who has transformed the conventional praise of Yahweh in Psalm 111 into a wisdom psalm that depicts the 'God-fearers' like himself as possessing God's attributes, than the other way round.

Psalm 112 is in a sense a Torah rather than a wisdom psalm, although the word *tôrâ* does not occur in it. Rather, it is the word 'commandments' (*miṣwôt*, v. 1, cf. Deut. 4.2; 11.1) that is used to designate the Law which is the delight of those who fear Yahweh. The theme of the psalm is precisely that of Psalm 1, which pronounces 'happy' (*ʾašrê*) those whose 'delight is in Yahweh's Torah' (Ps. 1.1a, 2a). Psalm 1 does not elaborate the details of the way of life of such persons as does Psalm 112; conversely, Psalm 1 devotes more space to the contrast with the wicked (vv. 4-5) than does Psalm 112 (v. 10). But undoubtedly Psalm 112 speaks the same language as Psalm 1 (and also as Ps. 119), in which obedience to the Law is both the fount of virtue and the source of blessedness.

Psalm 127

There has been considerable agreement among commentators that this psalm is in some sense wisdom literature (so, for example, Gunkel, Weiser, Kraus, Dahood). But if this is so, we find here a different kind of wisdom from that of the intellectual or introspective wisdom psalm.

Some commentators (Duhm, Gunkel, Briggs, Weiser) took Psalm 127 to consist of two completely unrelated parts, each a proverb or *Weisheitsspruch*, while others held it to be a unitary composition (so Barnes, Schmidt, Kraus, Dahood, Miller[31]). Schmidt's interpretation of the phrase 'builds a house' as meaning 'founds a family' made it possible to find a single theme here; this was accepted by Kraus, and also by Dahood, who pointed to a kind of *inclusio* (guarding the city, speaking in the gate), and by Miller, who, *inter alia*, pointed to a word play between *bānâ*, 'build', and *bānîm*, 'sons'. There is also a thematic consistency within the psalm, in that it expresses or implies the thought that nothing can be successfully accomplished without the help of Yahweh. The proverb-like style, however, does not qualify the psalm as a contribution to a late wisdom interpretation of the Psalter. Rather, whatever its precise *Sitz im Leben* may be, it should probably be seen as taking its place among the surrounding psalms which reflect everyday domestic concerns (Pss. 126 and 128).

Psalm 131

Gunkel classified this psalm as a psalm of confidence, a type that was an offshoot of the cultic lamentation. Like many, or even all, wisdom psalms it has a didactic intention, to present to the reader a model of the calm, confident person who stands in a right relationship with God. But it is also a personal statement or 'confession' by an individual about his own mental and spiritual state. Although it employs little specifically wisdom language (it is probably too brief for that), there is good reason for including it among the wisdom psalms. In v. 1 the psalmist boldly claims the virtue of humility: he does not busy himself with matters that are beyond him. It should be noted that modesty and humility, as contrasted with boasting, are important virtues characteristic of the wise, according to the wisdom teachers: cf. Prov. 15.33; 16.18, 19; 18.12; 22.4; 29.23, and other passages in Proverbs that condemn those who are 'wise in their own eyes' (3.7; 26.5, 12, 16; 28.11). A proud heart (*gābah lēb*) and 'haughty eyes' (*rāmû ʿênayim*) are also mentioned, and condemned, in Proverbs.

In v. 2 the psalmist explains how he achieved his modest and humble state: it was by exercising a deliberate control over his desires and ambitions, making himself like a little child. As Schmidt put it, he has

31. P.D. Miller, Jr, 'Psalm 127—the House that Yahweh Builds', *JSOT* 22 (1982), pp. 119-32.

learned to be content as he had not been before; restlessness and discontent are characteristics of fools (cf. Prov. 13.25; 30.15, 16). The psalmist's renunciation of 'great things' (*gedōlôt*, v. 1c)—that is, wealth, power, prestige—reflects the attitude of the wise man, who must not seek such things for himself, though he may be given them as a reward. We may therefore see this psalmist as an examplar of the wise man who has profited by the lessons of his teacher such as are found in the instructions of Proverbs 1–9. The final verse of the psalm is recognized by almost all commentators to be an addition similar to that with which Psalm 130 concludes (a psalm which has other affinities with Ps. 131), appended with the intention of transforming this private meditation into a nationally oriented prayer for the redemption of Israel.

Psalm 139

The *Gattung* of this psalm has proved notoriously difficult to define. Gunkel noted its hymnic element (that is, it is concerned with the praise of God), but saw it as unique in that it breaks out of the usual hymnic style, praising God not for his great deeds in past history but for his intrinsic nature. This is an intensely personal psalm which falls into a category of its own. Its spirit is that of Job and Ecclesiastes. Gunkel recognized that its interpretation depends on the question of its literary unity: all commentators have agreed that vv. 19-24 differ greatly in tone from vv. 1-18, and some (Briggs and Schmidt) argued that they are a completely independent poem. Gunkel, however, thought that the author of vv. 1-18 himself added the final verses to confirm with a tradition that hymns should conclude with the expression of wishes and petitions.

Among those scholars who maintained a single authorship for Psalm 139 some advanced the view that vv. 19-24, far from being an irrelevant appendage, provide the key to the interpretation of the whole psalm. Even Schmidt admitted that the repetition in v. 23 of the concept enunciated in v. 1 of God's 'examining' (*ḥāqar*) and 'knowing' (*yādaᶜ*) the psalmist suggests a possibility that the two parts share a common author, who, however, wrote in two different moods. Other commentators took this notion further. Several scholars (notably Dahood, Anderson, Koole[32], Würthwein[33]) postulated on the basis of vv. 19-24 that the psalm was

32. J.L. Koole, 'Quelques remarques sur le Psaume 139', in W.C. van Unnik and A.S. van der Woude (eds.), *Studia Biblica et Semitica T.C. Vriezen...Dedicata* (Wageningen: Veenman & Zonen, 1966), pp. 176-80.

33. E. Würthwein, 'Erwägungen zu Psalm cxxxix', *VT* 7 (1957), pp. 165-82.

composed for persons accused of idolatry (*ʿōṣeb*, v. 24) who were subjected to a test—perhaps through the device of the ordeal—and were obliged to defend themselves by declaring the orthodoxy of their beliefs. This theory was worked out in detail by Würthwein. He pointed out, however, that the psalm is not autobiographical: it was not composed by the accused, but written by a theologian on behalf of such people and for their use. Other scholars (such as Weiser and Wagner[34]) took the psalm more simply to be a wisdom piece of a didactic character, unconnected with any public or cultic ceremony.

Verses 1-18 comprise four sections. In vv. 1-6 the psalmist praises God's omniscience in personal terms: God mysteriously and wonderfully understands the writer's innermost thoughts. Verses 7-12 speak, still in personal terms, of God's omnipresence: however he tries, the writer cannot escape from him. Verses 13-16 return to the theme of omniscience, this time with reference to the psalmist's conception: God, who formed him from the womb, had complete knowledge of him even before he was born. Finally in vv. 17-18 the psalmist sums up all these thoughts, expressing his wonder at the vastness and multiplicity of God's mind (*rēʿîm*). As has already been noted, the final verses, after an impassioned denunciation of the wicked who hate God, resume the initial topic of God's examination of the psalmist's 'heart'.

Whatever may have been the occasion for which this psalm was written, it is a highly developed and mature account of God as creator, his universal knowledge and absolute power and his concern for every individual human being. Its themes are especially characteristic of the wisdom literature. The topic of God's intimate knowledge of the human heart is found frequently in Proverbs, especially in 15.11; 17.3; 20.24, 27; 21.1, and also in Job (see for instance 10.6, 14; cf. 14.16; 31.4). The thought that it is impossible for human beings to escape the scrutiny of God is of course not confined to the wisdom literature: it is a major theme of the book of Jonah and is also found in the prophetical books, for instance in Amos 9.2-3. But God's inescapability is also a feature of Job: Job constantly complains that he cannot escape from God's persecution (see for instance 7.19; 10.20), and Elihu points out (Job 34.22) that there is no place, however dark, where evildoers can hide from God; his words are reminiscent of Ps. 139.8-11. The description of the formation of a human child in the womb has only one parallel in the Old

34. S. Wagner, 'Zur Theologie des Psalms cxxxix', in J.A. Emerton *et al.* (eds.), *Congress Volume, Göttingen 1977* (VTSup, 29; Leiden: Brill, 1978), pp. 357-76.

Testament: Job 10.8-12. Both passages evince a 'scientific' interest peculiar to the wisdom books. Thus this psalm is a clear example of didactic wisdom writing, and this is so whether or not it was composed in the context of a need for individuals to defend the orthodoxy of their beliefs.

Conclusion

A considerable number of psalms have now been identified as wisdom or Torah psalms or as psalms that have been augmented in order to enable them to bear such an interpretation. It is clear that a particular group of those who recognized a need to reinterpret psalms for non-cultic use not only inserted new psalms of their own composition which expressed their own theology, but also remodelled other psalms for that purpose—although, as will be pointed out below, this can hardly have been the only respect in which reinterpretation was needed. It still remains to be discovered whether this wisdom and Torah reinterpretation was a systematic one—that is, whether one can speak of a completely wisdom- or Torah-oriented Psalter; whether the redactional activity in question can in fact be said to have corresponded with the final redaction of the whole Psalter. In view of the fact that the great majority of the Psalms appear to have been untouched by such manipulation, the answer to this question must lie, if anywhere, in the *placement* of the wisdom and Torah material in the Psalter: in other words, in its *structural* implications for the Psalter as a whole.

If it is conceded that the division of the Psalter into five Books may be in some way connected with its final redaction it is perhaps significant that by far the largest number of wisdom and Torah psalms or wisdom-oriented psalms occurs in Books I and V. There are twelve in Book I[35] and nine in Book V[36] as against two in Book II (Pss. 49 and 53), three in Book III (Pss. 73, 78, 86) and four in Book IV (Pss. 90, 92, 94 and 105). This might suggest that the final editors placed the greatest emphasis on the beginning and end of the book (perhaps first to introduce their reinterpretation of the Psalms to the reader and then finally to leave the reader with a strong impression of this reinterpretation); but it might equally suggest that it represents a failure to impose this interpretation successfully on the intervening material. On the other hand, there is some evidence that wisdom psalms were in some cases placed in particularly significant positions within individual Books. Apart from

35. Pss. 1, 8, 14, 18, 19, 25, 27, 32, 37, 39, 40.

36. Pss. 107, 111, 112, 119, 127, 131, 139, 144, 146.

Psalm 1, it is interesting to note that Psalm 73 stands at the beginning of Book III, that Psalm 90 similarly opens Book IV, and that Psalm 107 is the first psalm in Book V. It has also been noted that Psalm 73 stands at almost the central point of the Psalter.

It has also been suggested that the superscriptions that are attached to many of the Psalms, which were undoubtedly late additions to the text and not integral to it, may throw some light on the arrangement of the Psalter. However, there appears to be no evidence that particular groups of superscriptions are in any way related to the interpretation of the Psalter with which we are concerned here. Without undertaking a complete analysis of the superscriptions, the following facts may be noted. The wisdom psalms in Book I are all 'David' psalms; but that is also true of almost all the psalms in that Book (36 out of 41). These psalms belong to various *Gattungen* and share no common theme. Psalm 49, in Book II, is one of a series of 'Korahite' psalms (42, 44–49), while Psalm 53 belongs to a group attributed to the *m^enaṣṣēaḥ*, perhaps meaning 'director' (Pss. 42, 44–47, 49, 51–62, 64–70; Ps. 49 belongs to both groups). In Book III, both Psalms 73 and 78 are Asaph psalms (73–83), while Psalm 86 is a David psalm. In Book IV, Psalm 90 stands by itself as the only Moses psalm; Psalm 92 is assigned to the Sabbath; Psalms 94 and 105 have no superscription. In Book V the wisdom psalms are variously attributed: Psalms 111, 112 and 146 are hallelujah psalms; Psalms 127 and 131 are found among the Songs of Ascents, but Psalm 127 is also attributed to Solomon and Psalm 139 both to the *m^enaṣṣēaḥ* and to David. Psalm 144 is a David psalm, and Psalms 107 and 119 have no superscription. There appears to be no discernible pattern in the superscriptions, and no principle seems to have been operative in the case of the wisdom psalms. This is also true of the superscriptions in the LXX, which differ to a considerable extent from the MT and thus complicate the matter of a 'final redaction'. It has been noted that Psalm 119 stands immediately before the Songs of Ascents, but it is not easy to see what structural significance this may have had.

It is universally agreed that certain groups of psalms were formed before the final editing of the Psalter took place. The final editors sometimes preserved these groups intact, but this was not invariably the case: some appear to have been subsequently broken up. There are, for example, several distinct groups of consecutive psalms attributed to David which may once have belonged together; and among these it is significant that the twelve psalms whose superscriptions associate them with incidents in David's life—an example of a very distinctive editorial principle—are, with one exception (the juxtaposition of Pss. 51 and 52), not now placed, as might be expected, together or even in close proximity but are scattered throughout the Psalter. A similar situation is observable in the case of the Korahite psalms and to some extent of the Asaph psalms. The Songs of Ascents, on the other hand, constitute a solid group that has remained intact, although the reasons for their juxtaposition are not entirely apparent.

The existence of other groups of psalms formed prior to the final redaction of the Psalter can also be detected; again, there has been fragmentation. Thus psalms that begin or end with 'hallelujah' may be presumed to have once belonged together, but they now constitute distinct groups. A group of psalms praising Yahweh as king, Psalms 93–99, which (with the exception of Ps. 98) lack superscriptions, has been recognized as a distinct group by modern scholars; but within this group also there is one psalm (Ps. 94) which is of a totally different genre and thus splits the group.

These phenomena, which point to editorial confusion rather than to systematic activity, no doubt attest the complexity of successive processes of redaction that led to the formation of the Psalter as we now have it, processes that may have been undertaken in some cases with mutually contradictory intentions. In the total absence of direct evidence it is unlikely that it will ever be possible to unravel and fully describe and account for those processes. It is clear, however, that in the final stage of compilation, and probably also in the earlier stages, one of the most difficult editorial tasks was to decide how best to make use of the material that had already been formed into groups in a way that accorded with particular editorial interests. Our concern here is to investigate whether the hands of those whose aim was to impose a new interpretation on the Psalms on the basis of wisdom and Torah principles can be traced in the Psalter in its final form.

Wisdom Psalms and their Contexts

Various attempts have been made by recent scholars to show that in some cases wisdom psalms were placed in their present contexts in order to give a wisdom interpretation to immediately adjacent psalms or to small groups of psalms. Some of these proposals will now be considered.

Psalms 84–88

Psalms 84–88 constitute a group of psalms attributed to the sons of Korah, with the exception of Psalm 86. This is a David psalm, and splits the group in the middle so that it now consists only of two pairs, Psalms 84–85 and 87–88. As has been noted above, Psalm 86, although not originally a wisdom psalm, has subsequently been given a wisdom orientation by the addition of v. 11, in which the interpolator recognizes his inadequacy and prays for instruction (*hôrēnî*) in Yahweh's way (*derek*) so that he may lead his life in faithfulness (*ʾemet*) to him, and may be given a heart to fear his name. It is possible that the addition of this verse was intended not only to give a more humble orientation to this psalm, in which the psalmist makes the confident assumption that he is *already* numbered among those who faithfully praise and glorify God with their whole heart (so v. 12), but also to administer a similar 'correction' to the other psalms in this group.

Psalms 84–85 and 87–88 differ in their genres, but like Psalm 86 in its original form they exhibit in their various ways their authors' confidence that they are persons worthy of God's acceptance. Psalm 84 expresses the sentiment that simply to attach oneself wholeheartedly to the temple is a sufficient guarantee of God's favour (see for instance vv. 3, 5, 8, 11); the author claims to derive his strength from God (v. 6) and to be of blameless life (v. 12). In Psalm 85 the psalmist similarly claims to qualify for divine favour as one of Yahweh's *ḥᵃsîdîm* who turn to him in their hearts (v. 9) and fear him (v. 10); his petition is simply that Yahweh will now 'show' (*harʾēnû*) to his faithful people his *ḥesed* as in former times (vv. 7-8). Psalm 86 (apart from v. 11) employs similar language (see for example vv. 2, 4, 5). The author of Psalm 87 makes no such explicit claim but only speaks of the wonder of Zion and of his love for it; but the psalmist in Psalm 88 again speaks of himself as one who is entitled to be a recipient of Yahweh's help (v. 2), though he cannot understand why this has been withdrawn from him. Only in Ps. 86.11 in all this group of psalms is there a recognition that only by attending to Yahweh's instruction is it possible to achieve true reverence for Yahweh and true obedience to his will. It is, then, possible that Psalm 86 in its final form was intended to 'correct' or reinterpret the assumptions made in this group of psalms about the psalmists' unquestioned right to appeal confidently to Yahweh for his help.

Psalms 92–99

It is also possible that the placement of Psalms 92 and 94, both of which are wisdom-oriented in their present form, constitutes a deliberate reinterpretation of a group of psalms that had been formed previously. Psalms 93–99, a group known as 'enthronement psalms', are interrupted by Psalm 94, and Psalm 92 stands immediately before this group. The group mainly lacks superscriptions in the MT: only Psalm 92 has an extended superscription, designating it a psalm for the Sabbath; Psalm 98 is headed simply by 'A psalm' (*mizmôr*). In the LXX, however, all these psalms have superscriptions, all of which (except that of Ps. 99) include an ascription to David. But it is their theme rather than their superscriptions that defines them as a group.

In this case it is probably more appropriate to speak of the wisdom elements in Psalms 92 and 94 as complementary to the ideas of the other psalms in the group than as 'corrections' to them. Psalms 93–99 are cultic psalms praising Yahweh as king, creator of the world and sole ruler, and they make comparatively few specific references to the present situation of the worshippers, although Psalms 95 and 99 contain warnings based on the past sinful history of the people. Psalm 94, immediately following Psalm 93 which confines itself entirely to statements about Yahweh's kingship and the holiness of the temple, interrupts the sequence with references to the wicked who persecute his people and to their eventual destruction, and then in vv. 8-11 emphasizes the need to heed divine teaching in order to understand the fact that Yahweh observes and punishes them. There is then further teaching in vv. 12-15 on the good fortune that will be enjoyed by those who receive that instruction. Thus in its present form Psalm 94 balances the cultic euphoria of Psalm 93 with reflections on the current plight of the worshippers and the need to learn the practical implications for God's people, a lesson that is equally applicable to the rest of this group of psalms. The lesson is reinforced by Psalm 92, which in vv. 6-8 similarly warns that Yahweh's thoughts are 'very deep' (*m*^{e}*ʾōd ʿām*^{e}*qû*) and beyond the comprehension of the stupid.

Psalms 105–107

These psalms also form a thematic group in that they all recount Yahweh's dealings with his people in the past and the present. They all lack superscriptions in the MT, but the first two are linked in that both end with 'hallelujah' (Ps. 106 also begins in this way). In the LXX Psalm 107 has a superscription ascribing it to David. It is interesting to note that the group cuts across the division into Books: Psalm 107 begins Book V, a fact that suggests that the division was subsequent to the formation of the group.

The three psalms are chiastically arranged. Psalms 105 and 107, both of which have been oriented to wisdom/Torah by their final verses, enclose Psalm 106, which contains no such orientation. There is also a chiastic arrangement as regards theme: Psalms 105 and 107 are chiefly concerned with Yahweh's deeds performed on behalf of Israel or of human beings in general rather than with their reactions to those deeds, while Psalm 106 is as much concerned with the people's sinful behavior as with Yahweh's anger and mercy. Psalms 105 and 107 end similarly, with warnings respectively to keep Yahweh's laws and to learn from his kindly behaviour. These two final verses thus provide a comment on the whole group of psalms, especially Ps. 107.43. This final verse of the group, calling on anyone who is 'wise' (*mî-ḥākām*) to observe or lay to heart 'these things' (*w^{e}yišmor-ʾēlleh*) and to consider Yahweh's love (*ḥas^{e}dê yhwh*), clearly refers to all that has been said in these psalms about him. Here, then, is a case not of interrupting a coherent group with an additional psalm but of pointing a wisdom moral at its conclusion.

Psalms 111 and 112

The similarity of the wisdom psalm 111 and the Torah-related psalm 112 has already been noted. These two psalms form an independent pair—a fact that points to the close relationship between wisdom and Torah theology.

A 'Wisdom Book'?

The above observations suggest that in a number of instances wisdom and Torah psalms have been deliberately placed so as to reinterpret adjacent psalms or even a whole group of psalms. But the larger question of *systematic* placement of such psalms so as to form a 'wisdom book' or a book designed as a single work for consecutive reading remains to be considered. In this connection it is especially relevant to discuss the frequently debated question of the relationship between Psalms 1 and 2.

Psalms 1 and 2

The relationship between these two psalms is a crucial question for theories of a systematic redaction of the whole Psalter. There is evidence from the Talmud and elsewhere that these two psalms were treated as one by some authorities from an early period; this cannot, however, be regarded by itself as proof that they were in fact composed as a single unit, or even that they have been edited in such a way as to make them so. Recently new arguments have been put forward to show that such a link does exist, though these have been disputed by others (notably Anderson, Willis[37] and Murphy[38]).

Following the now widely held view that Psalm 1 constitutes the introduction to the whole Psalter (see below), or at least of Book I, hitherto unsuspected affinities between that psalm and Psalm 2 have been postulated. A similarity between the first verse of Psalm 1 and the last phrase of Psalm 2 has been noted and dubbed an *inclusio*: Ps. 1.1 speaks of the happiness of those who reject the counsel and the ways of the world, while Ps. 2.10-12 warns rulers to be wise (*haśkîlû*) and to serve and fear Yahweh; further, in both 1.6 and 2.12 the key words *derek*, 'way', and *ʾābad*, 'perish', occur in similar contexts of Yahweh's anger and judgment. Auffret further claimed that the two psalms share a common literary structure.[39]

In addition, a thematic affinity has been postulated: both psalms, it has been argued, are constructed on the basis of the motif of the contrast between the 'two ways' and the fates of those who pursue them—the wicked and the righteous in Psalm 1, and the nations of the world with their kings and Yahweh and his anointed king in Psalm 2 (so, for example, Lipiński[40]). Mays concluded from this similarity that Psalms 1 and 2 *together* form the introduction to the Psalter: Psalm 2 will have been interpreted in an eschatological sense, and placed in its present position in order to give an eschatological reinterpretation of Psalm 1: 'The end of the wicked and the vindication of the righteous can be understood in terms of the coming kingdom of God.'[41] Miller expressed a somewhat similar view.[42] Craigie suggested that the two psalms were placed together to provide a 'double perspective'. Another indication that

37. J.T. Willis, 'A Cry of Defiance—Psalm 2', *JSOT* 47 (1990), pp. 33-50.

38. 'Reflections', pp. 22-23.

39. P. Auffret, *The Literary Structure of Psalm 2* (JSOTSup, 3; Sheffield: JSOT Press, 1977), pp. 31-34.

40. E. Lipiński, 'Macarismes et psaumes de congratulation', *RB* 75 (1968), pp. 330-39.

41. J.L. Mays, 'The Place of the Torah-Psalms in the Psalter', *JBL* 106 (1987), p. 10; see also 'The Question of Context', pp. 16-17.

42. 'The Beginning of the Psalter'.

the two psalms were intended to be read together and that they stand apart as a closely connected pair has been seen in the fact that Psalm 2 almost alone among the Davidic psalms 2–41 has no superscription.

Other scholars have denied the existence of any special connection between the two psalms. The immediate impression that the reader receives from reading them together is one of total dissimilarity. Psalm 1 breathes the rarified atmosphere of the wisdom or Torah instruction; it is entirely lacking in references to specific events or situations in the real world. No account of the nature of the wicked (*rᵉšāʿîm*, v. 1) is given; rather, their role is simply that of negative foils to those who follow and delight in Yahweh's Law. Psalm 2 on the other hand deals with the turmoil of the real world, in which foreign kings conspire against and attack Yahweh's chosen king whom he has set on Zion and to whom he has promised the destruction of his enemies. However this psalm is to be interpreted, whether as referring to a particular historical situation when Israel's existence was threatened by foreign enemies or as expressing expectation of an eschatological event, it is specific and concrete in its imagery. The warning in vv. 10-11 to the kings of the nations to listen to reason (*haśkîlû*) and to accept the reality of their situation by submitting to Yahweh's sovereignty in order to escape destruction may be seen as a rhetorical appeal to the absent kings which has little in common with the wisdom instruction, despite the use of a verb commonly found in the wisdom literature. The final line of the psalm, pronouncing 'happy' (*ʾašrê*, v. 12) those who take refuge in Yahweh, is not really comparable with the *ʾašrê* pronouncement in Ps. 1.1: the verb *ḥāâ*, 'to take refuge', in the same verse is characteristic of the Psalms in general (it occurs 24 times in the Psalter), but is found only twice in Proverbs and not at all in the other wisdom books. To take refuge in Yahweh is not a wisdom concept.

Opposing the view that Psalms 1 and 2 are closely connected, Anderson suggested that the occurrence of a 'two ways' motif in both psalms might well be coincidental. This view has some plausibility. Although the key terms *derek* and *ʾābad* occur in both psalms, the wider contexts indicate that one psalm is unlikely to have influenced the other. Furthermore, the doctrine of the two ways is not confined to the wisdom literature but is found frequently in other parts of the Old Testament, especially (but not only) in Deuteronomy (Deut. 28 is an extended exposition of it) and the Deuteronomistic History. It may almost be said to be one of the central principles of Old Testament ethics.

Willis dealt with the question of the combination of the two psalms as one in relation to ancient tradition.[43] He pointed out that this was by no means a universal understanding, and cited the witness of the early Church Fathers, almost all of whom regarded them as separate psalms. Murphy, in a critique of the views expressed by Mays in the same volume, advised great caution in the matter;[44] he pointed out the hypothetical nature of Mays's view, concluding that his case fell short of plausibility. In view of these differences of opinion it is probably unwise to use the hypothesis of the unity of Psalm 1 + 2 as a basis for an understanding of the composition of the Psalter.

Links between Adjacent Psalms

It was the contribution of Reindl, made at the IOSOT Congress of 1980 and subsequently published in the Congress Volume in 1981,[45] that initiated the search for indications of links between pairs or groups of adjacent psalms. Some of the results of the search have been less plausible than others. Reindl, who put forward the view that the psalms have been editorially arranged with the view of creating a book that could be used by readers for the purpose of private study and edification, stressed the importance of Psalms 1 and 150 as constituting a framework for the book, and then proposed some examples of the arrangement of groups of psalms within that framework, using the criteria both of theme and of shared terminology. With regard to the conclusion of the Psalter he argued that Psalms 146–150, although they do not formally all belong to the same genre, are linked together by the key word 'hallelujah' and by their common theme of the praise of Yahweh, but also in other ways, especially by common elements of vocabulary. They are all to be regarded as expansions of the simple call to praise Yahweh, and so constitute a block of psalms that express the primary goal of all worship, together making a fit conclusion to the Psalter, summed up in the final words of Psalm 150: 'Let everything that breathes praise Yahweh!'

As an example of a similarly linked group of psalms within the body of the Psalter Reindl cited Psalms 90–92. He pointed out that these psalms are all concerned with the human condition, although they belong

43. J.T. Willis, 'Psalm 1—An Entity', *ZAW* 91 (1979), pp. 381-401.

44. 'Reflections', pp. 22-23.

45. 'Weisheitliche Bearbeitung von Psalmen'.

formally to different *Gattungen* and speak of this in different ways. They all make use of wisdom terms and have a didactic tendency, and they are linked by the occurrence of identical words even in the non-wisdom passages: *mā‘ôn*, ‘dwelling’ (90.1; 91.9), *ʾelyôn*, ‘Most High’ (91.1; 92.2) and *po‘olekā*, ‘your works’ (90.16; 92.5). The three psalms in their present order lead the reader from the thought of the ephemeral nature of human life (Ps. 90) through an expression of confidence in Yahweh’s protection (Ps. 91) to one of thanksgiving that he has in fact provided that protection for the righteous. Reindl’s analysis of these three psalms has great plausibility, although his argument from vocabulary is, by itself, hardly convincing. However, the evidence that he has offered from these and some other groups of psalms is not sufficient to support his thesis that there was a systematic ordering of the whole Psalter in wisdom terms, especially as he himself admitted that the examples that he offered are not necessarily the work of the same editor.

Howard attempted to identify a much more extensive group of psalms, having Psalms 90–92 as its centre but having links also with Psalms 88–89 and 93–100 and even with Psalms 101–106.[46] He categorized Psalms 88 and 89 as psalms that doubt or question God, and interpreted Psalm 90 in more positive terms than Reindl had done, seeing its affirmation of God’s faithfulness to the covenant (v. 1) as forming a bridge to the ‘towering affirmations’ of the psalms that follow. He also found a link between Psalms 92 and 93 in their references to Yahweh’s eternity and ‘high position’, expressed in the words *mārôm* and *le‘ōlâm* in 92.9, *mē‘ôlām* in 93.2 and *mārôm* in 93.4. But his statement that Psalm 93 depicts Yahweh as one who ‘gives the faithful the confidence to face their own conditions and ask God for help’[47] is to read into the text something that is simply not there.

Such attempts to force psalms into a pattern of meaning that does not exist in the text illustrate the great danger of subjectivity in psalm interpretation and also show how a psalm that contains mixed, not to say contradictory, statements can be interpreted quite differently depending on the stress that is placed on particular verses. The impression is given that with a sufficient amount of ingenuity it would be possible to find links between almost any pair or group of psalms selected at random.

46. D.M. Howard, Jr, ‘Contextual Reading of Psalms 90–94’, in J.C. McCann (ed.), *The Shape and Shaping of the Psalter* (JSOTSup, 159; Sheffield: JSOT Press, 1993), pp. 108-23..

47. Howard, ‘Contextual Reading’, p. 114.

More recently Lescow has postulated a close link between Psalms 24, 25 and 26 in terms of Torah and wisdom.[48] Taking Psalm 24 as a Torah psalm (in a somewhat unusual sense) because it lists ethical conditions prescribed for admission to worship at Yahweh's holy place, he drew attention to the fact that Psalm 26 appears to be a kind of 'reverse image' of it. Psalm 26 is an expression of the self-justification of one who takes an oath of purification, claiming that he has in fact fulfilled the conditions set out in Psalm 24, or at least somewhat similar ones: particularly, the possession of 'clean hands' (*n*ᵉ*qî kappayim*) of 24.4a has its counterpart in the 'I wash my hands in innocence' (*ʾerḥaṣ b*ᵉ*niqqāyôn kappāy*) of 26.6, and 'who has not lifted up his soul in impiety' (*ʾ*ᵃ*šer lōʾ-nāśâ laššāwʾ napšô*) in 'I do not sit with the impious' (*lōʾ-yāšbtî ʿim-m*ᵉ*tê-šāwʾ*) of 26.4. Lescow does not, however, suppose that these two psalms were composed as counterparts to one another: each had its own independent origin and history. It was a late editor who used them to form a group of psalms together with the late acrostic Psalm 25 in a ring-formation or *inclusio*. His argument thus depends on the presentation of evidence of links existing between Psalm 25 and its two neighbours.

Psalm 25, as has already been noted, is a pure wisdom psalm. Lescow bases its relationship to Psalms 24 and 26 to a large extent on the repetition of key words: *nāśâ* in 24.4, 5, 7, 9 and 25.1; *tōm*, 'integrity', in 25.21 and 26.1, 11; *nepeš* in 24.4; 25.1, 13, 20 and 26.9; *lēb* in 24.4; 25.17; 26.2; and on the notion of 'walking' (*hlk*) in Psalms 24 and 26 and the frequent occurrence of *drk*, 'way, lead', in 25.4, 8, 9, 12, which he defines as a key word in that psalm, though it occurs neither in Psalm 24 nor in Psalm 26. All these words are of course fairly frequent in the Psalms, but they are used in various quite different senses here. The notion that Psalm 25 is used as a bridge between Psalms 24 and 26, showing how the fulfilment of Yahweh's requirements in Psalm 24 could be achieved as in Psalm 26 by means of learning from Yahweh's ways and accepting his guidance is not without some plausibility, but the argument is far from being convincing.

Conclusion

Although some of the proposals discussed above lack plausibility, the existence of the phenomenon of wisdom and Torah influence on the

48. T. Lescow, 'Textübergreifende Exegese: Zur Lesung von Ps 24–26, *ZAW* 107 (1995), pp. 65-79.

Psalter cannot be doubted. It is equally clear, however, that there is no tangible evidence of a consistent and systematic attempt to link the whole collection of psalms together by editorial means. There is, however, another method by which the Psalter may be shown to have a kind of literary unity. This does not require a minute examination of each psalm and its relationship with its neighbours, but is concerned with a much broader treatment of the material. It is well known that one effective way of reinterpreting collections of heterogeneous literary material used by ancient Near Eastern and Old Testament scribal editors was to enclose such material within an introduction and a conclusion to the whole work. An example of the use of such a method with regard to a biblical book is Proverbs, where the initial chapters (1–9) and the final poem (31.10-31) have been placed in their positions for such a purpose, while also having at least occasional links with parts of the intervening material which, in this way, they attempt to reinterpret. That this may be true of Psalms 1 and 146–150 has been noted above.

In the case of Proverbs, however, the reinterpretive process is easier to comprehend than in the case of the Psalter. The book of Proverbs is wholly concerned with a single topic: wisdom; that is, with the quality that enables men and women to behave in a manner that conduces to social harmony and to prosperity. The only matter on which the different parts of the book differ in their teaching is the *nature* of wisdom: whether, for example, it comes as a gift from God or whether it is simply a question of common sense. If we may assume that the initial verses of Proverbs provide the reader with hermeneutical spectacles through which to view the rest of the book, there would be no need here for a drastic reinterpretation of the material. The whole book is about wisdom, and the introductory verses simply direct the reader to a particular interpretation of it. In the Psalter, on the other hand, the programme set out in Psalm 1 would require the reader to understand all the liturgical texts that follow in an entirely new and unaccustomed way: it would, for example, necessitate the reading of specific references to animal sacrifice as metaphors for the spiritual life.

That such a spiritualization of the Psalter did take place is an undoubted fact: the works of Philo, for example, are an outstanding example of this, and it is a practice that has never been discarded. But there is no textual evidence supporting an intention to apply this principle to every psalm, and it cannot be shown that Psalm 1 provides a clear message to readers that they are to do so for themselves. The theory of a reorientation of the whole Psalter through its introductory and concluding verses is unable to account for the apparently random way in which the Psalms have been ordered. The placing of the Torah psalms 19, 73 and 119 as guides along the way, as it were (so, for example, Westermann, 'Zur Sammlung des Psalters') hardly seems to constitute an adequate means to keep readers from straying from the 'right' way of reading the Psalter, even if the central position of Psalm 73 has some especial significance.

Some scholars have concentrated on the different Books of the Psalter in an attempt to understand editorial intentions with regard to those parts of it. Such a study may shed light on penultimate or earlier stages of composition, a matter that has its own importance, but it cannot contribute to the understanding of the Psalter as a unitary work unless some indications can be found that the distinct Books, or other distinct collections within the Psalter, have been editorially linked. This matter was first raised by Wilson in *The Editing of the Hebrew Psalter*; he postulated a general 'progressive' scheme with the 'seams' of the various parts having been 'stitched up' for this purpose. He argued that Books I–III are concerned with David and the Davidic dynasty and its failure under David's successors, and Book IV with the implications of this failure, while Book V offers a hopeful answer to these problems based on a belief in Yahweh's kingship. This rather bland characterization of the various Books does not account for the many psalms that could, according to Wilson's own characterization of their themes, have equally been placed elsewhere.

Brueggemann's attempt to see a 'theological intentionality' running through the Psalter from beginning to end in terms of a movement from obedience to praise is made on somewhat similar lines but on a less specific basis. That Psalm 1 calls for an obedience to God's Law that is also a delight and that the Psalter ends with the expression of pure praise in Psalm 150 is a correct observation. In this article[49] Brueggemann does not attempt to demonstrate in detail what specific parts in the progression from obedience to praise are played by all the remaining 148 psalms, but contents himself with a sketch of the issues of crisis, despair, hope and faith in the life of Israel and of the individual that they reflect, issues that are also applicable to the personal experiences of the later intended readers. It is this rather loose application of the notion of 'progression' in the flow of the Psalter that may have greater plausibility than the more

49. 'Bounded by Obedience and Praise'.

precise attempts to account for the placing of particular psalms. However hard one may try to account for the arrangement of the Psalter, it is difficult to dismiss the impression of randomness in the positioning of many of them.

Up to this point the question that has been posed is whether the Psalter in its final form is the product of a post-exilic redaction whose intention was to make it into a book designed to be read privately for edification by individuals. Many of the psalms, as we have seen, do not obviously bear the marks of such an orientation. This raises the question, assuming that the evidence for a wisdom redaction is valid, whether that redaction was in fact the final one.

The history of the composition of the Psalter is an extremely complex one which has not been, and probably never will be, completely understood. Many scholars would agree with this judgment. The text of the Psalter itself contains no direct statement relevant to the process of its composition except for the note in Ps. 72.20 which states that the prayers of David son of Jesse are ended. The fact that a number of smaller collections within the Psalter have been identified shows that its redaction was not carried out in a single act. The division into five Books is evidently ancient since it is found in the LXX as well as in the MT, but it cannot be identified with any particular stage of the redaction of the book, and indeed may have been somewhat later than the final redaction of the text. The same is true of the superscriptions attached to many psalms. Some of these, for example, must be the work of persons who intended the psalms to which they are attached to be seen as inculcating lessons drawn from historical incidents in the life of David.

But the practice of wisdom and of obedience to the Torah cannot have been the only preoccupation of members of the post-exilic Jewish communities. For example, if we may assume with most scholars that at least the majority of the psalms that refer to the king were originally intended to be understood literally—that is, as referring to the actual king of Israel or Judah at the time of their composition—it is clear that some reinterpretation of those psalms would have been necessary if they were to retain some relevance to a later community; and it is probable, in view of undoubted eschatological and messianic interpretations of the Davidic monarchy attested in some of the prophetical books from the time of the exile onwards, that in some cases at least this would have been an eschatological interpretation. Since the wisdom literature of the Old Testament shows no interest in eschatological speculation, it is improbable that such an interpretation would have been the work of wisdom or Torah redactors; and if it can be shown that some of the royal psalms bear the marks of an eschatological interpretation, we are faced with a quite separate redactional stage of composition from that which has been discussed above. The evidence for such redactional activity will now be considered.

Chapter 3

ESCHATOLOGICAL INTERPRETATION

Royal Psalms

It may first be remarked that some scholars have been cautious about accepting that there is a distinct eschatological orientation of royal psalms within the Psalter, and have interpreted these psalms in other ways. It is, for example, an obvious fact that such psalms, especially those in Book I whose superscriptions attribute them to incidents in the life of David, have, at some late editorial stage, been given not an eschatological interpretation but a 'historical' one: the historical David is represented as a pious person who prayed to Yahweh to help him in trouble and duly thanked him when he had been delivered from danger. This indicates a homiletic intention well within the compass of a 'wisdom' redaction of the Psalter, since its purpose was to instruct the pious reader.

Other recent scholars, however, have focused their attention on royal psalms that are more susceptible of an eschatological reading. McCann, for example, suggested that Psalms 2, 72 and 89 give the collection a future orientation;[1] on the other hand, the effect of their placement—with Psalm 89, with its picture of Yahweh's rejection of both king and people placed last—was 'to document the failure of the Davidic covenant' (as Wilson had already argued[2]). Books IV–V (Pss. 90–150) could then be seen as giving the answer to this failure: those final books stress the sovereignty of Yahweh alone. Wilson argued that there are two distinct notes in the Psalter, that of royal covenant and that of wisdom, the two constituting a dialogue in tension corresponding to a tension in the lives of the post-exilic community.[3] But it was the wisdom teaching that finally prevailed in the Psalter: readers were eventually discouraged from

1. 'The Psalms as Instruction', pp. 122-23.
2. *The Editing of the Hebrew Psalter*, pp. 207-14.
3. 'Shaping the Psalter', pp. 80-82.

continuing to long for a restoration of the Davidic dynasty (in whatever form) and encouraged to place their hopes in a kingdom not of this world where Yahweh alone is king.

Psalm 2

The opinion that this psalm was composed in conjunction with Psalm 1 or alternatively that the two psalms were originally a single work has been considered above and rejected. Nevertheless it is a psalm of particular importance for a discussion of the editing of the Psalter, especially in view of its prominent position. As has been noted above, some early authorities referred to it as 'the first psalm', and the suggestion that there was a time in the editorial process when it functioned as the introduction to the Psalter, or at least to the 'Davidic' psalms (Briggs, Kraus, Miller[4]) should not be disregarded: it might thus have provided a hint of the way in which other psalms should be regarded. Since its placing can hardly have been accidental, it could have been intended to encourage an eschatological or messianic reading.

In Ps. 2.6 Yahweh states that he has placed his king on Zion, his holy hill. It is now generally believed that this refers either to a particular (unnamed) king of Judah or (if the psalm was intended to be used at the accession of each new monarch) to any Judaean king. In v. 2 it is stated that the kings of the earth have conspired to attack Yahweh and his anointed one (*māšîaḥ*). In v. 7 Yahweh recognizes the king as his son, and in v. 8 he promises to give him world dominion. The king, then, is represented in this psalm as associated with Yahweh and as deriving his universal authority from him.

The meaning of these grandiose statements requires clarification. As has been pointed out above, they are reminiscent of a situation which occurred not infrequently in the imperial states of the ancient Near East. There the death of the king frequently led to uprisings among vassal states, with which the newly appointed monarch had to deal (cf. Ps. 2.2) by asserting the continuation in his person of the divinely conferred power over the nations that had belonged to his predecessor. Since, however, no Israelite king can reasonably be said to have exercised such imperial power, the statements made in Psalm 2 may be said to be examples of a hyperbolic 'court style' whose claims in fact always exceeded reality, since not even Near Eastern imperial rulers dominated

4. Miller, 'The Beginning of the Psalter', pp. 85-88.

the whole world. Used of a king of Judah they were particularly remote from reality.

But they raise an important question. It might be that in claiming universal power for the reigning king the psalmist is saying no more than that since the king has been appointed to be a representative and even an agent of the omnipotent Yahweh, such world dominion is a real possibility for Judah. His statements would then be expressing a hope for an ideal future, but an immediate one: a hope that the new king would prove to be an ideal ruler—perhaps a new David. On the other hand, the psalmist might have had a more remote future in mind: world dominance for Judah under an ideal ruler yet to come. Such a messianic interpretation would be a natural one to be adopted by a post-exilic people whose only present king was a foreign ruler, although there is nothing in the text that requires this. Nor has any of the commentators suggested that the text has been expanded or modified to facilitate such an interpretation.

Psalm 18

It has been noted above that Psalm 18 has been embellished with wisdom elements, especially in vv. 26-30. But is it possible that it has also been given a messianic interpretation? It is generally agreed—with the exception of those who have regarded the psalm as a deliberate combination of two originally separate psalms—that the speaker is, or at least is represented as, an Israelite king, possibly David. This is of course asserted by the superscription; but there is also abundant evidence of it in the text (for example, the reference to military victories in vv. 38-43 and the claim to have won dominion over foreign peoples in vv. 44-49). But in the present text, whether original or added in the interests of reinterpretation, there are signs that the king in question is no ordinary human being.

Vesco regarded the psalm as a kind of midrash or haggadic exegesis based on traditions about David.[5] A passage which is quite astonishing, whether the psalm is regarded as an individual thanksgiving with the king as speaker or as a victory song, is the theophany in vv. 8-16. Little attention has hitherto been paid to this. The king prays to God for help in his trouble, and Yahweh replies with a full-scale theophany reminiscent of the scene on Mount Sinai, in which Yahweh blasts the enemy with

5. 'Le psaume 18, lecture davidique'.

earthquake, smoke, fire, darkness, thunder and lightning until the very foundations of the earth are laid bare. Why should this be? Such drastic behaviour on Yahweh's part is inconceivable if it is performed on behalf of an ordinary mortal, even a king like the historical David; and to say that the description is merely metaphorical is an equally inadequate explanation.

Something very remarkable is happening here; and it would be natural for the post-exilic reader, despite the apparently present tenses employed in the description of the theophany, to read these verses as at the very least speaking of a 'new David' greater than the historical David. The final verse, which is regarded by some commentators as an addition to the original psalm, may be an expression of hope in the coming of this new David. The perfect tenses have now given way to participles: Yahweh makes, or will make, great (*magdîl*) the triumphs or victories (*yᵉšûʿôt*) of his king, and will show his love or faithfulness (*ḥesed*) to his anointed one. Whether the final line is a further addition, as some have suggested, is not clear: but that is probably immaterial.

Psalm 45

This psalm has been regarded as in some sense 'messianic' by both Jewish and Christian exegetes. The Targum, followed by subsequent Jewish interpreters, saw it as speaking of the marriage of the future Messiah, with the people of Israel depicted as the bride. Christian interpreters, beginning with the author of the Epistle to the Hebrews (1.8-9), identified the king of whom the psalm speaks with the person of Christ. The view unanimously held by modern exegetes is that the psalm is a song from the time of the monarchy celebrating the marriage of a historical king of Israel (which of these is not agreed) with a foreign princess.

Verses 7-8 are a clear allusion to the promise made to David that his dynasty would continue for ever (cf. 2 Sam. 7.11-16 and certain other passages in the Psalms), and in that sense it has a 'messianic' character. But the question to be raised here is whether there is any evidence in the text itself of changes or additions made in the post-exilic period to further expectations of the restoration of the Davidic monarchy. In fact no such evidence is apparent. In v. 8 the king is ostensibly addressed as 'God' (*ʾᵉlōhîm*), and this has given rise to many attempts to account for this unique appellation or to explain it away.

The identification of the king with God—if that was the intended meaning—would hardly be congenial to Jewish orthodox beliefs, although it was used by later Christian exegetes for a christological purpose. Thus, although a messianic interpretation of the psalm as a whole began quite early, there is no evidence that it played a part in the history of the text itself. (The LXX does not differ significantly from the MT in v. 8.)

Psalm 72

The position of this psalm at the end of Book II together with that of another royal psalm (Ps. 89) at the conclusion of Book III tends to confirm the suggestion made above, about Psalm 2 and the Davidic superscriptions in Book I, that the editors of these three Books were concerned to bring the Davidic monarchy into special prominence. The present psalm's superscription (*lišᵉlōmōh*) and its editorial appendix, 'The prayers of David son of Jesse are ended' (v. 20), further confirm this. The whole psalm—apart from the doxology in vv. 18-19—is a prayer for the king and may have been written for his coronation. The hyperbolic language of some verses, especially vv. 5-11, which express a wish for the king's eternal reign (v. 5; not the eternal reign of the dynasty but of the individual named in v. 1 as *melek* and *ben-melek*), for life-giving influence like that of the rain falling on the earth (v. 6), and above all for universal dominion (vv. 8-11), is such as to point beyond the present to a future saviour-figure (so Kraus). Earlier commentators (notably Duhm and Briggs), stressing that these characteristics go beyond anything to which an Israelite king could aspire, regarded vv. 5-11 or part of them as a late interpolation expressing a messianic hope. More recently it was pointed out that this language has close affinities with Sumerian, Akkadian and Ugaritic royal texts embodying a concept of sacral kingship which the psalmist, probably in conformity to current ideas, took over (so especially Kraus, who nevertheless held that this does not exclude the possibility of a future reference; cf. also Jacquet and Anderson). It is now generally accepted that the verses in question are not an interpolation but are integral to the psalm, which is probably pre-exilic; but the psalm's present position suggests that this pre-exilic 'messianism' was adopted and given prominence by editors of a later period.

Psalm 89

This psalm is complex and cannot be fitted into a single *Gattung*. Kraus's formal analysis is representative of the commentators: vv. 2-19 are a hymn, vv. 20-38 a divine oracle and vv. 20-52 a lament. But in dynamic terms there are only two 'episodes': the glorious past and the lamentable present. That the psalm is composite in that the psalmist has incorporated various items of (probably) pre-existent material may be agreed; but the claim that part or parts of it come from different periods, or, more radically, that it is an amalgamation of two or more originally separate psalms (as proposed by Duhm, Gunkel and Schmidt) is disproved by the existence of many links between its various parts. It has been welded into a literary unity. The most obvious of the above-mentioned links is the pervading theme of the king and his dynasty.

Verses 2-19, which praise Yahweh both for his love and faithfulness and for his righteous rule over the world, purport to cite the words that he spoke when he established his covenant with David and promised him an eternal dynasty (vv. 4-5); the final verse of this section (v. 19) forms a link with the second part by means of a reference to the reigning king, who is the protector ('shield') of the people but who is himself empowered and protected by God. Verses 20-38 consist of a second and much more extended divine oracle concerning David and his descendants which, like the first one, purports to be a citation of Yahweh's original promise. The major and devastating break in the psalm occurs at v. 39: this lament (vv. 39-52) accuses God of having completely broken his promise, renounced his covenant and removed the king in defeat from his throne. Verses 47-52, while reproaching God for his faithlessness, implore him even now to remember his former love for his servant.

Whatever may have been the national defeat that occasioned the composition and performance of this psalm—whether the destruction of Jerusalem in 586 BCE or some earlier defeat (the theory of a liturgical ceremony in which the king was subjected to ritual humiliation is now discredited)[6]—it is hardly correct to see it in its present position in the Psalter as having been used editorially to document the failure of the Davidic monarchy and the unlikelihood of its restoration, as some scholars have done (notably McCann and Howard). It is important to bear in mind that laments in the Psalter, whether individual or national, are not expressions of despair. However much the psalmists may accuse God of breaking his word and becoming an enemy, hope always remains that intercession will be effective: hence the characteristic 'How

6. See, e.g., S. Mowinckel, *The Psalms in Israel's Worship*, I (Oxford: Blackwell, 1962), pp. 242-43).

long?' (usually *ʿad-matay*, here *ʿad-māh*, v. 47) and 'Will you hide yourself for ever?'. Even in apparently hopeless circumstances, and despite the bitterness of their tone, the psalmists continued to hope. So here in Psalm 89 the psalmist urges God not to forget the promises that he has made that the Davidic dynasty would be for ever (vv. 5, 22, 29, 30), and stresses his faithfulness in passages to which he gives such prominence that they cannot have been intended merely as foils for the account which follows of disillusion and consequent loss of faith.

This has been recognized by several commentators and other scholars. Barnes considered the psalm to have been composed in the early post-exilic period when some still hoped for the restoration of the Davidic monarchy (cf. also Anderson). Weiser spoke of the psalmist's faith in an inscrutable God, even though he had deliberately broken his covenant, as a severe lesson to be learned. Kraus, though he also spoke of the incomprehensibility of God's action, referred to his promise as ultimately unbreakable. Van der Ploeg[7] also commented that there is clearly a hope here that the psalmist's prayer will be answered. There is in fact every reason to suppose that the psalm has been placed here not as a demonstration of the failure of the historical Davidic dynasty but as an expression of a hope that Yahweh's *ḥesed*, so prominently shown in the past to David, will again be exercised in favour of his downtrodden people, although there is no trace here of 'messianic' additions to the text.

Psalm 110

The placing of this psalm makes it difficult to accept the view that, following the demonstration of the failure of the Davidic monarchy in Books I–III, the compilers of the Psalter moved on, beginning with the psalms of Yahweh's kingship (Pss. 93–99), to present the readers with the proposition that Yahweh alone is the true king in whom they should put their trust. Here in the final book we find a royal psalm that presents a particularly positive picture of the Davidic king empowered and protected by Yahweh. In recent times there has been a widespread scholarly consensus that it comes from a relatively early period of the Israelite monarchy. It is often regarded as having been composed for the coronation of a Judaean king, though this view is disputed by some (see,

7. J.P.M. van der Ploeg, 'Le sens et un problème textuel du Ps lxxxix', in A. Caquot and M. Delcor (eds.), *Mélanges bibliques et orientaux en l'honneur de M. Henri Cazelles* (AOAT, 212; Kevelaer: Butzon & Bercker; Neukirchen–Vluyn: Neukirchener Verlag, 1981), pp. 471-81.

for instance, Kraus and van der Meer[8]). Some have questioned its unity, especially in view of the fact that it contains not one but two divine oracles (vv. 1, 4).

The psalm is much concerned with military matters: that is, with Yahweh's action, on the king's behalf, in defeating and destroying his enemies (this motif occurs in vv. 1, 2, 3, 5 and 6). It is this concern that led van der Meer to see it as addressed to or spoken on behalf of a king not at the time of his accession but at a time when he had been defeated, deprived of his throne, and exiled (as, for example, was David during Absalom's rebellion, 2 Sam. 15–19): it promises his restoration and rehabilitation.

But in view of the relatively early messianic interpretation of this psalm in the New Testament, where it was understood christologically,[9] some scholars have been led to enquire whether an eschatological or even messianic meaning was originally intended. That much of the hyperbolic language used here about the king is representative of a common Near Eastern view of monarchy is generally accepted. Other features such as the reference to Melchizedek in v. 4 probably go back to early Israelite traditions. The figure of Melchizedek, although its only other occurrence in the Old Testament is in Genesis 14, probably belongs to an early tradition that linked the Davidic line of kings with the pre-Israelite priest-kings of Jerusalem, while the assertion that the Davidic kings were also priests reflected the fact that they did in fact perform priestly acts and were responsible for cultic arrangements, as were the kings of the surrounding peoples.

But it has been plausibly argued that Psalm 110, even in its original pre-exilic form, looked forward beyond the fortunes of the contemporary line of Israelite kings to some future divine consummation of God's sovereign rule over the world. This view is based on the cumulative evidence of certain expressions and lines that transcend the 'court style' referred to above. One of these is Yahweh's command to the king to sit at his right hand (v. 1), which may mean to share Yahweh's sovereignty, coupled with the word 'until' in that verse, which clearly refers to a future consummation. Another is the LXX text of v. 3, which reads: 'I

8. W. van der Meer, 'Psalm 110: A Psalm of Rehabilitation?', in Van der Meer and J.C. de Moor (eds.), *The Structural Analysis of Biblical and Canaanite Poetry* (JSOTSup, 74; Sheffield: JSOT Press, 1988), pp. 207-34.

9. Mt. 22.24; 26.64; Mk 12.36; Lk. 20.42-43; Acts 2.34-35; Eph. 1.20; Col. 3.1; Heb. 1.13; 5.6; 6.20; 7.17-21.

have begotten you from the womb before the morning'—a phrase that goes mysteriously beyond Ps. 2.7.

But the most important evidence is to be found in vv. 5b-6, which refer to Yahweh's 'day of wrath', his judging (*dîn*) of the nations and his wholesale slaughter carried out throughout the 'wide world' (*ʾereṣ rabbâ*). These lines have been seen as anticipating a final cosmic judgment. It should be noted that they make no reference to the king: they refer to Yahweh alone. Verse 7, however, reverts to the king; the break is an awkward one, as the 'he' of v. 7 ought logically to refer to Yahweh, though in fact it is obviously a statement about the king. Kraus remarked about these verses that 'the acts of the earthly king have been incorporated into the mighty going forth of God in the "day of his anger"'. It is perhaps more true to say that the notion of Yahweh's eschatological action has been incorporated into a psalm about the earthly king, so creating the possibility of understanding vv. 5b-6 as an eschatological insertion into a prior royal context, enabling the king to be seen as the future messianic ruler.

Kraus was not the only modern scholar to sense that this psalm is concerned with a future expectation rather than solely with the immediate present. Weiser commented that in vv. 5-6

> the person of the king and his enthronement are lost behind the exclusive activity of God...It was this perspective that also suggested the possibility of a purely eschatological interpretation of the whole hymn on the lines of God's judgement on the whole world being the Last Judgement and the person of the king being interpreted as the Messiah.

Van der Meer expressed a somewhat similar view.

Psalm 132

This unusual psalm is supposed by most modern commentators to have accompanied a ceremony such as a feast of dedication of the First Temple. Its *Gattung* is difficult to determine. It may be that different voices are speaking. The psalm brings together three related themes: the Ark, Yahweh's choice of David and his dynasty, and Yahweh's choice of Zion, the site of the temple, as his abode.

The psalm begins in vv. 1-7 with a prayer to Yahweh to 'remember' David and his determination to find a dwelling-place for him, and continues with a reference to the discovery of the Ark and with the expression of a desire to go to worship at the dwelling-place that has now been chosen. Verses 8-10 appear to presuppose a somewhat different situation in which Yahweh and his Ark are situated outside the temple and are about to move in procession to his resting-place, accompanied by the priests and a joyful crowd; an appeal is then made to Yahweh to accept the worship of his anointed one (*m*^{e}*šîḥô*)—presumably the reigning king—for David's sake (v. 10 clearly points back to v. 1). That Yahweh ought to be favourable to the king is then further supported by the citation of the oath that Yahweh had sworn to David to ensure the eternal succession of his descendants provided that they obey him and keep his covenant (vv. 11-12). The next section of the psalm (vv. 13-16) is concerned with Yahweh's choice of Zion as his dwelling; and again a promise of Yahweh is cited, this time to bless and prosper priests and people. Finally (vv. 17-18) there is a further promise by Yahweh of prosperity and success for his anointed one.

The psalm refers to David by name four times: in vv. 1, 10, 11 and 17. In the first three of these it is ostensibly the historical figure of King David that is, at least primarily, intended: he is remembered as the one who found the Ark and brought it to its resting-place in Jerusalem, and as the one to whom Yahweh had promised an eternal—though conditional—dynasty and his continued favour. In v. 10, then, it seems most natural to interpret the 'anointed one' as the current reigning monarch. However, it has been suggested that the psalm is messianic at least in its present form: that it looks not for the continuation of the present dynasty but for its revival after its historical demise. The verses that have been particularly held to express this expectation are vv. 17-18. Of the older commentators, Briggs suggested that these verses may be a later appendix to the psalm, looking forward to a future messianic king 'from the point of view of one who knew nothing of the monarchy in his own time'.

This has not been the opinion of subsequent commentators. Recently, however, Kruse has argued that the whole psalm is post-exilic.[10] In his opinion v. 5 cannot refer to the Tent, but must refer to the Jerusalem temple; and it is only in the late post-exilic books of Chronicles that we find it stated that David, though he did not build the temple, chose the site and made all the preparations for its construction and furnishing. Yahweh's promise to provide for the poor, not found in earlier versions of his promise to David, also presupposes a post-exilic situation in which most of the inhabitants of Jerusalem could be described as poor.

10. H. Kruse, 'Psalm cxxxii and the Royal Zion Festival', *VT* 33 (1983), pp. 279-97.

The petition in v. 10 in this context is to be seen as a prayer for the swift coming of the messiah; the reference in the psalm to the Ark in v. 8b reflects the tradition preserved in 2 Macc. 2.7-8 and attributed to the prophet Jeremiah, where he is said to have prophesied that God will appear in glory together with the long-absent Ark when he gathers his people together and shows his mercy to them (an elaboration of Jer. 3.16-17). The statement that the Ark was found at Ephrata is reminiscent of the post-exilic Mic. 5.1, which prophesies the coming of a ruler for Israel.

Not all of the points made by Kruse are convincing, though his understanding of the psalm remains a possibility. But the most important argument that he put forward concerns vv. 17-18, in which he saw a clear—though symbolic—prediction of the coming of the messiah. His argument about the significance of these verses, especially v. 17, is a strong one. Yahweh there promises to cause a horn to sprout 'for David' (*šām ʾaṣmîaḥ qeren lᵉdāwīd*) and to 'prepare a lamp for my anointed one' (*ʿāraktî nēr limᵉšîḥîʾ*). This is messianic language. These lines have an unmistakable affinity with Jeremiah's *ʾaṣmîaḥ lᵉdāwīd ṣemaḥ ṣᵉdāqâ* ('I will cause to spring up a righteous branch', Jer. 33.15; cf. Ezek. 29.21, *ʾaṣmîaḥ qeren lᵉbêt yiśrāʾēl*), and with Jer. 23.5, *wahᵃqīmōtî lᵉdāwīd ṣmaḥ ṣaddîq*, 'and I shall raise up for David a righteous branch', which is followed by 'and he shall reign as king and deal wisely'. *ṣemaḥ* is also used of a future leader in Zech. 3.8; 6.12. In this context the parallel line should be taken similarly. The phrase 'I will prepare a lamp for my anointed one' recalls the designation of David as the 'lamp of Israel' in 2 Sam. 21.17, and this may have become a stock epithet for the reigning Davidic king; but the phrase 'I shall prepare' (or, 'I have prepared', *ʿāraktî*) used in this connection strongly suggests a single crowned figure (*wᵉʿālâw yāṣîṣ nizrô*, v. 18) to appear in the future. There is, therefore, good reason to suppose that vv. 17-18 of this psalm, if not the whole psalm, express a messianic hope of a new David to come.

Conclusion

Of the royal psalms considered above some perhaps show signs of having been textually adapted to express some kind of hope for a 'new David' under whom the Davidic monarchy, now historically defunct, would be revived. Others may have been composed especially with that intention. Others again, of earlier origin, lend themselves easily to such an interpretation and were probably understood in that way from an early date. Three—Psalms 2, 72 and 89, especially the first of these—have been placed in prominent positions which support the notion of an orientation along messianic lines. There are also other psalms with royal features that have not been considered here—Psalms 20, 21, 28, 61, 63, 78, 144—which do not lend themselves very obviously to messianic interpretation, but could perhaps do so in the context of a more general tendency in the minds of persons who were looking for such a meaning. There is no evidence that redactors set themselves deliberately to document the failure of the Davidic monarchy and to draw theological conclusions from this: rather the contrary. The setbacks experienced by various kings are not concealed; but this did not, apparently, exclude hopes, so frequently expressed in many of the royal psalms, for the fulfilment of God's promise to David in an eschatological future. This phenomenon is paralleled in some of the prophetical books.

At the same time it is clear that there was no *systematic redaction* of royal psalms, any more than there was a systematic wisdom redaction. The most that can be said is that the hope of a restoration of the monarchy under a royal figure was alive for some during the post-exilic period and that some expression was given to this in the Psalms, though not usually by means of textual additions and interpolations.

This kind of theological thought hardly seems compatible with the wisdom or Torah theology present in some other psalms; we must, then, acknowledge the existence of (at least) two different theological impulses operating within the doubtless very complex and still largely unknown process of the composition of the Psalter. Certainly to speak of a 'wisdom Psalter' is to make a considerable overstatement.

Chapter 4

The Interpretation of Ritual Sacrifice

Prominent among the themes which editors of the Psalter might be expected to have thought it necessary to reinterpret or modify for the post-exilic reader is that of sacrificial worship. As is well known, the necessity or validity of animal sacrifice is seriously questioned in a number of passages in the prophetical books (Hos. 6.6; Amos 5.22, 25; Mic. 6.6-8; Isa. 1.11; Jer. 6.20) and also in 1 Sam. 15.22, where Samuel is represented as stating that Yahweh does not take pleasure in animal sacrifice and that obedience to God is the essential requirement. However, the dating of these passages is uncertain, and many scholars have argued that their authors' intention was not to oppose the practice as such: they were concerned only to make the point that sacrifice was not the sum total of God's requirements of his people and that obedience to his moral commands was more important. Consequently there is no certainty as to whether there was a party in pre-exilic times that rejected the sacrificial cult. The meaning of the early post-exilic Isa. 66.1-4, which may be a contemporary comment on the proposed building of the Second Temple and the intended resumption of the sacrificial system, is obscure. But there is reason to believe that after that temple was built in the late sixth century BCE and ritual sacrifice was resumed and practised with even more intensity than before, the belief arose in some circles—not necessarily only in the Diaspora—that sacrificial worship was inessential or even mistaken, and that the Second Temple period saw a marked development of alternative forms of worship, though the temple may have retained some importance for those people as a house of prayer.[1]

1. See most recently R. Albertz, *A History of Israelite Religion in the Old Testament Period* (London: SCM Press, 1994), II, pp. 508, 520-23 (ET of *Religionsgeschichte Israels in alttestamentlicher Zeit* [Göttingen: Vandenhoeck & Ruprecht, 1992], II); also L.L. Grabbe, *Judaism from Cyrus to Hadrian* (Minneapolis: Fortress Press, 1992; London: SCM Press, 1994), I, pp. 18-19, 103-104, 108-109, 129.

We are thus entitled to enquire whether in the text of the psalms that refer to sacrificial worship there is evidence of editorial activity that questioned its validity or necessity. The wisdom and Torah psalms are silent on this matter, and this silence might be taken to show that animal sacrifice did not figure in the minds of their authors and editors as part of the spiritual life of worship and praise. But there are many psalms that express a very positive attitude towards sacrifice as an essential part of worship, as something to be taken for granted; and it would surely be expected that if there had been a thorough anti-sacrificial redaction of the Psalter its redactors would have found it necessary to modify or reinterpret these passages by giving them a figurative or spiritualized meaning. There is in fact no evidence of such a wholesale redaction. The many psalms that express an intense devotion to the temple have been left untouched, and this is also true of most of the psalms which more specifically refer to sacrifice in the temple as an essential part of worship.[2] That such psalms were interpreted in a spiritualizing sense by some readers, as in postbiblical times, must be regarded as certain; but only in a few cases can it be argued that modification or reinterpretation is to be found in the text itself. These psalms will now be examined.

Anti-Sacrificial Reinterpretations?

Psalm 40

Almost everything about this psalm is disputed. Formally it consists of an individual psalm of thanksgiving (vv. 2-11) followed by an individual lament (vv. 12-18, of which vv. 14-18 are virtually identical with Ps. 70). In view of this unusual sequence, many commentators have regarded the psalm as the result of a combination of two originally separate psalms; but others (Weiser, Craigie and Ridderbos[3]) argued that it should be understood as a royal liturgy in which the king, having given thanks for Yahweh's favour in the past, then presents his appeal for help in his present situation.

Particularly controversial are the verses that refer to sacrifice (vv. 7-9), in which the psalmist (or the king) states that Yahweh does not require sacrifice, but on the other hand speaks of his delight in doing God's will and of God's 'law' (*tôrâ*) being in his heart. Schmidt and Weiser interpreted v. 7 as a total repudiation of sacrifice, though Schmidt saw v. 8 as

2. For example, Pss. 4.6; 20.2-4; 27.6; 54.8; 66.13-15; 118.26-27.
3. 'The Structure of Psalm xl'.

a subsequent addition in which an adherent of a contrary party pointed out that the Torah itself prescribes sacrificial worship. More recently Anderson and Craigie, following Mowinckel,[4] argued that the intention of vv. 7-9 is to reinterpret the notion of sacrifice as a part, but only a part, of God's requirements of his servants.

Verses 7-9 in fact present a number of problems of detailed interpretation. Following the initial statement that God does not take pleasure in sacrifice and offering (*zebaḥ ûminḥâ*) occurs the confession that he has 'dug ears for me' (*ʾoznayim kārîtā lî*), usually taken to mean that he has *opened* the speaker's ears. Dahood interpreted this as meaning that God has made him receptive to a divinely inspired message, presumably conveying what God's demands really are. These words, which are introduced without a connecting particle and which also fall outside the metrical pattern, may be an interpolation (Kraus): v. 7b reverts to the statement at the beginning of the verse, repeating it except that it now states that God does not require burnt offering (*ʿôlâ*) or sin offering (*ḥᵃṭāʾâ*, probably another form of the more usual *ḥaṭṭāʾt*). That there is textual corruption here seems clear.

The speaker then exclaims in v. 8 'Behold, I have come' (*hinnēh-bāʾtî*), apparently indicating a kind of self-offering (Kraus thought that the speaker was presenting himself as the offering), followed by the words 'in the scroll of the book it is written concerning me'. The 'book' in question has been taken by some scholars to mean the written Torah, especially in view of the further statement in v. 9b, 'your *tôrâ* is in my inmost self (*tôrātᵉkā bᵉtôk mēʿāy*), that is, in his heart. This interpretation of 'book' and '*tôrâ*' is, however, very uncertain. Craigie argued that the 'scroll of the book' in question which is written 'about me' refers to the law of the king in Deut. 17.19-20, according to which the king is to learn to fear God and obey him, and that this is implied in v. 9 in which the king expresses his delight in doing God's will.

Other interpretations have been suggested. Anderson, however, concluded that there is insufficient evidence in this difficult passage to determine what is meant. If indeed the 'book' and '*tôrâ*' do refer to the written Law, this would mean that the psalm (or at least these verses) is basically a Torah psalm which at the same time appropriately rejects sacrificial worship. But it would be rash to draw this conclusion from a text whose meaning remains obscure.

4. *Psalmenstudien*, VI, p. 51.

However, it should be pointed out that vv. 7-9 of this psalm fit into a pattern found elsewhere deprecating animal sacrifice. This pattern consists of two basic elements. First, there is a denial that God requires or takes pleasure in sacrifice, expressed in one or both of two verbs (or their cognate nouns) meaning 'to take pleasure (in something)' or 'to be favourable'. These are *ḥāpēṣ* (with *ḥepeṣ*), which occurs in Ps. 40.7; 51.18; Isa. 1.11; Hos. 6.6; 1 Sam. 15.22, and *rāṣâ* (with *rāṣôn*), in Ps. 40.7; 51.18; Jer. 6.20; Amos 5.22; Mic. 6.7. The second element is a statement of what God really requires, expressed more variously but in closely related terms: obedience to his will (Ps. 40.8-9; Jer. 6.19; 1 Sam. 15.22), repentance (Ps. 51.18; Isa. 1.16-17), just and moral behaviour (Isa. 1.16-17; Amos 5.24; Mic. 6.8), humility (Mic. 6.8) and the knowledge of God (Hos. 6.6).

Some commentators (Schmidt and Kraus) have expressed doubts about the integrity of vv. 7-9 and their relation to the rest of the psalm. It may be significant that it is precisely in these verses that there are textual difficulties. It is possible that they have been interpolated into the psalm (i.e. into vv. 1-11) to emphasize that the experience of deliverance from near death suffered by the speaker (vv. 2-4) was not, and indeed never is, contingent on the offering of sacrifice. It should be noted that vv. 7-9 do not interrupt the thought and that their omission would leave no unexplained gap in it. The speaker has praised Yahweh for his deliverance in a 'new song', and then generalizes his experience: all who trust Yahweh will attain blessedness (*ʾašrê*). Verse 10 follows v. 6 without any necessity for a reflection on the validity of sacrifice. The final line of v. 6 has frequently been misunderstood as expressing an inability to give a full account of God's saving actions (RSV has '*Were I to* proclaim and tell of them'); but the literal sense is 'I will make known (*ʾaggîdâ*), and I will speak' (JB has 'I would proclaim...but they are more than I can tell'). Verse 10 then continues the theme: Yahweh knows that the psalmist has never failed to proclaim his righteousness (or 'saving acts') in the great congregation. There is no mention of sacrifice elsewhere in the psalm; rather, it is trust in Yahweh that results in a state of blessedness (v. 5).

Psalm 50

The section of this psalm that deals with the question of animal sacrifice (vv. 8-15) has rightly been compared with the denunciations of sacrifice in the pre-exilic prophets (Isa. 1.11-17; Hos. 6.6; Amos 5.21-24; Mic. 6.6-8). It has raised the same question in the minds of the commentators:

is this an outright condemnation, or is it directed only against a misunderstanding or misuse of the practice? Here the answer to this question depends to some extent on the view taken of the character of the psalm as a whole and of its original setting. Some commentators have described the setting only in general terms ('didactic poem' [Briggs]; 'liturgy' [Weiser]; 'prophetic judgment liturgy' [Kraus]); others consider that it was composed for use at a particular (cultic) festival. Craigie saw it as a liturgy for the renewal of the covenant, at which sacrifices would undoubtedly have been offered.

Despite the vehemence of the language of vv. 8-15, some of which taken at face value might seem to reject the offering of sacrifice altogether, the great majority of commentators have agreed that these verses imply no more than that animal sacrifice is unacceptable to God only when there is a misunderstanding of its true purpose. In vv. 9-15 God himself is presented as declaring his true nature—as opposed to false notions, evidently still at least tacitly held, that God, who has the whole created universe at his disposal, nevertheless needs to receive gifts of animals from his worshippers (vv. 9-11), or that, like the gods of other nations, he experiences hunger and would eat their flesh and drink their blood. These notions are dismissed as ludicrous.

In contrast, the psalm describes the nature of true and acceptable worship. Here, however, the language used is not entirely clear. In v. 14 we find the command *z*^{e}*baḥ lēʾlōhîm tôdâ*. Although *tôdâ* by itself can mean simply 'thanksgiving' or 'song of thanksgiving', the normal meaning of the verb *zābaḥ* is 'to slaughter (an animal sacrificially)', and *tôdâ* is often closely associated with the sacrifice itself. These considerations would favour the translation of this line as 'Slaughter for God a sacrifice of thanksgiving'. Similarly in v. 23 *zōbēaḥ tôdâ y*^{e}*kabb*^{e}*dān*^{e}*nî* would mean 'the person who offers a thanksgiving sacrifice honours me'.

The view that vv. 8-15 do not reject animal sacrifice itself but only a wrong understanding of it is generally thought to be supported by v. 5. There Yahweh is described as summoning his faithful people (*ḥ*^{a}*sîdîm*) to meet him for judgment, and he there calls them 'those who made the covenant with me by [or with] sacrifice' (*kōr*^{e}*tê b*^{e}*rîtî* ^{ca}*lê-zābaḥ*). Here it is clear that *zebaḥ* refers literally to animal sacrifice, and for the psalmist that is a sign of the covenant and an essential feature of its ratification (cf. Exod. 24.8, where the blood of the slaughtered oxen is called 'the blood of the covenant'). Verse 5 of this psalm thus presents a problem for those who hold that vv. 8-15 express a total rejection of animal sacrifice. Gunkel simply remarked that the verse is 'inconsistent' with the rest of the psalm. Schmidt, who was alone in regarding the psalm as composite, attributed v. 5 and vv. 8-15 to different authors.

In sum, it may be said that although the psalmist may not have intended to condemn animal sacrifice altogether, an anti-cultic reader would have been able to interpret the psalm in that way if 'sacrifice of thanksgiving' were understood figuratively (see below on Ps. 51.19). It is not certain how v. 5 would have been understood by such a reader; it might perhaps have been regarded as a unique exception.

Psalm 51

The great majority of commentators, together with other scholars,[5] were of the opinion that the final two verses of this psalm (vv. 20-21) are not part of the original psalm but a later addition to it. The main ground for this opinion is that their positive attitude towards animal sacrifice conflicts with, or at least seeks to modify, the original psalmist's apparent rejection of all animal sacrifice in vv. 18-19. Only Briggs, Barnes and more recently Dahood have supported the literary integrity of the whole psalm. The question thus turns mainly on the interpretation of vv. 18 and 19. Is the psalmist's declaration that God has no delight (*lōʾ-taḥpōṣ*) in the sacrificial slaughter (*zābaḥ*) of animals and will not accept a burnt offering (*ʿôlâ lōʾ-tirṣeh*) but will accept the 'sacrifice' of a broken spirit and heart (*zibᵉḥê ʾᵉlôhîm rûaḥ nišbārâ*) a categorical rejection of animal sacrifice? Alternatives to this interpretation were considered by a number of commentators but rejected. On the other hand Briggs and Barnes argued that in vv. 18-19 the psalmist, owing to his awareness that he had committed a particularly grave sin (such as rebellion against God), was here stating that *for him* sacrifice was not sufficient to make atonement: it was available and efficacious only for those whose lesser sins had already been pardoned by God after confession. He himself, in those circumstances, sees that his only hope lies in a direct appeal to God. Dahood appears to have taken a similar view: he compared the language of v. 18 with that of Yahweh's denunciation of the neglectful and dishonest priesthood in Malachi: 'I have no pleasure in you, says Yahweh of hosts, and I will not accept an offering *from your hands*' (*ʾên-lî ḥēpeṣ bākem...ûminḥâ loʾ-ʾerṣh miyyedᵉkem*, Mal. 1.10).

5. For instance E.R. Dalglish, *Psalm Fifty-One in the Light of Ancient Near Eastern Patternism* (Leiden: Brill, 1962), pp. 201-208.

On the other hand, it is important to note that in affirming that the 'sacrifices' that are acceptable to God are a broken spirit and a humbled heart (v. 19), the psalmist is using the word *zebaḥ* in an entirely new, provocative and unique way which contrasts strongly with his conventional use of it in the previous verse, where it stands in parallel with *ʿôlâ*, 'burnt offering'. What the psalmist is doing in v. 19 is deliberately paradoxical: *zebaḥ* in the conventional sense is not acceptable to God; but he will accept *zebaḥ* if it consists of a humble heart, for which the psalmist has prayed in v. 12. It is relevant to ask whether this new sense of *zebaḥ* should be regarded as no more than a literary device employed by this writer alone, or whether it is evidence of the beginning of the development of a new usage among those who opposed animal sacrifice. This question will be considered below, especially with reference to the expression *zebaḥ/zib*ᵉ*ḥê tôdâ* and comparable expressions in Pss. 50.14, 23; 107.22 and 116.17.

The interpretation of vv. 20-21 as expressing an unconditional *approval* of sacrifice is likewise not without problems. Verse 21 asserts that God *will* (or expresses the hope that he *may*) delight in sacrifices, but emphasizes that these must be 'right' sacrifices (*zibeḥê-ṣedeq*); and v. 20 appears to state that this will not be a possibility until (*ʾāz*, 'then') he chooses to rebuild the walls of Jerusalem (the historical situation reflected here is generally presumed to be that of the period between the destruction of Jerusalem in 587 BCE and the activity of Nehemiah). Despite these reservations, however, v. 21 can only be interpreted as recognizing in principle the desirability and effectiveness of animal sacrifices. The author of these verses clearly looks forward to a time when they will again be offered and acceptable (*ʾāz taḥpōṣ zib*ᵉ*ḥê-ṣedeq*).

The strongest argument in favour of the view that vv. 20-21 are a later addition to the psalm is, however, not their approval of sacrifice. It is rather to be found in the abrupt change of theme and tone between v. 19 and v. 20, from personal private confession to communal hope. Duhm's comment that the final two verses 'have nothing to do with the psalm' appears fully justified in purely structural terms. However, the fact that the words *ḥāpēṣ*, *zebaḥ* and *ʿôlâ*, which occur in v. 18, all reappear in v. 21 can hardly be fortuitous. Whether vv. 20-21 were composed as an addition to the psalm, or are an independent piece subsequently attached to it, it is reasonable to suppose that their author or redactor inserted them to correct a possible understanding (or misunderstanding) of vv. 18-19 as totally opposed to animal sacrifice. At all events, the psalm in its final form concludes with a forthright endorsement of the practice, which does not support the view of those who might have wished in some way to spiritualize it.

Psalm 69

Some older commentators (notably Duhm) considered this psalm to be the result of the combination of two originally distinct psalms; but all the more recent critics have regarded it as a single psalm. Gunkel identified it as an individual lamentation which changes to a psalm of thanksgiving in v. 31, a view which has since commanded universal assent. Kraus, following Begrich,[6] accounted for the change of tone by assuming that a priestly oracle of salvation had intervened between the lament and the thanksgiving.

The only specific reference to animal sacrifice in the psalm occurs in vv. 31-32, where the psalmist states his intention to praise God with a song and to honour him with a *tôdâ*. As has already been noted, this term can denote either a sacrifice or a song of thanksgiving; but in v. 32 the psalmist makes it clear that he means the latter, stating 'This will please Yahweh more than a bull (*w^{e}tîṭab l^{e}yhwh miššôr*) or than a young bull with horns and cloven hooves'—that is, more than the most costly of sacrificial offerings. There is no reason to suppose that these verses are a later interpolation into the psalm. (Anderson suggested that there is a play on words here, pointing to the contrast between *šôr*, 'bull', and *šîr*, 'song'.)

It is not certain what is meant by v. 10a, in which the psalmist refers to his zeal for Yahweh's 'house' (*bêtekā*). This may depend on the date of the psalm, which is also uncertain; some hold it to have been composed during the exile, when there was no temple in existence. But it seems clear that, though the psalmist evidently believed that his thanksgiving song would be more acceptable than an animal sacrifice, vv. 31-32 should not be interpreted as necessarily reflecting a total rejection of the latter. However, these verses were certainly susceptible to such an interpretation, and the psalm as a whole strongly emphasizes the efficacy of prayer. The psalm would thus have been entirely acceptable to those who rejected animal sacrifice, and an editor holding those views would not have thought it necessary to make any 'corrective' changes to the text.

6. J. Begrich, 'Das priesterliche Heilsorakel', *ZAW* 52 (1934), pp. 81-92.

Psalm 141
There is a reference in v. 2 of this individual lament to the sacrificial rites of the temple. The psalmist prays that his prayer may be accepted 'as' incense (*tikkôn t*ᵉ*ppillātî qetōret l*ᵉ*pānêkā*) and 'as' an evening sacrifice (*maśᵓat kappay minḥat-ᶜāreb*; cf. 2 Kgs 16.15). These are terms that normally refer to the regular performance of the temple ritual. Incense was employed as an accompaniment to the grain offering (see for instance Lev. 2.1, 15) but may have accompanied animal sacrifice as well.[7] *minḥâ* was the regular term for the grain offering, but it could also denote the whole sacrificial system.[8] *kûn* (*niphal*, here in the imperfect, *tikkôn*) appears in Chronicles in connection with the service of the temple (see for instance 2 Chron. 35.10, 16); but here it probably has the less specialized sense of 'stand, be established': the psalmist is asking that his prayer may in some sense 'stand for' or take the place of the temple ritual as an effective means of atonement (so Gunkel, Schmidt, Weiser, Kraus, Dahood, Allen).

The commentators are generally agreed that no rejection of ritual sacrifice as such is implied here. The reason why the psalmist cannot participate in the temple ritual is not stated, but it is evident that this is the case. Instead, it appears that he deliberately makes his prayer at the normal hour of the evening sacrifice (cf. Exod. 29.41 and Daniel's daily prayer towards Jerusalem, Dan. 6.11).

But the commentators are not entirely agreed as to whether the verse should be taken to imply a view that sacrifice, though not wrong, is unnecessary: that prayer is *in principle* an adequate substitute for it. This might point to the existence of a section of the population of Jerusalem and its environs who, though the temple was in existence and its rituals regularly carried out, were indifferent to sacrifice and practised a strictly non-cultic form of piety. Duhm postulated a custom of domestic prayer which took the place of sacrifice; Weiser took a similar view. But others (notably Dahood and Allen) held to the view that in the case of Psalm 141 the psalmist had in some way been *prevented*—by reason of distance from the temple or from some other cause—from participation in the temple rituals whose importance and efficacy he did not doubt.

7. See M. Haran, 'The Uses of Incense in the Ancient Israelite Ritual', *VT* 10 (1960), pp. 113-29.

8. See A. Marx, *Les offrandes végétales dans l'Ancien Testament*, in J.A. Emerton (ed.), *Congress Volume* (VTSup, 57; Leiden: Brill, 1994), especially pp. 1-28.

There has, however, been a general consensus that v. 2 does mark a degree of 'spiritualization' of sacrificial worship, in that private prayer was accepted at least in some circumstances as able to take its place. Since the verse could be interpreted as promoting the value of private prayer as against ritual sacrifice no further comment would have been needed from a redactor who wished to further such a view.

Of the five psalms considered above, only Psalm 40 may have been augmented by a redactor who wished to make the point that animal sacrifice was not required by God of those who wished to do his will. In the other four instances, in all of which the value of sacrifice is discussed, there are ambiguities which might have made it possible to interpret these passages along anti-sacrificial lines, though this is not true of Psalm 51 in its final form. But the Psalter as a whole is unquestionably a book that speaks very frequently, and with obvious approval, of the temple and what is done there. Not only do very many psalms express delight in Zion and in Yahweh's 'house'; specific positive references to sacrifice itself are frequent. In these psalms there is no discussion of the value or importance of sacrifice; rather, this is assumed and taken for granted as an essential and normal feature of worship. It is noteworthy that there is no evidence, and indeed no reason to suppose, that any redactional activity has taken place in the text of these psalms that might be taken to reflect an anti-sacrificial attitude.

Positive Attitudes to Sarifice

Psalm 4

In this psalm the psalmist calls on the people to 'offer right sacrifices' (*zibḥû zib^{e}ḥê ṣedeq*) and to trust God (v. 6). As in Ps. 51.21 *ṣedeq* probably means 'right' in the sense of what is acceptable to God (cf. Deut. 33.19), implying that this is not always the case. In view of v. 6b and vv. 2-3 'right sacrifices' probably means sacrifices offered by those who have abandoned the 'vanity and lies' that dishonour Yahweh, and have turned to him in trust. Verses 5 and 6 are overloaded, and it has been supposed that v. 6 is redundant. However this may be, there is no reason to suppose that the reference to sacrifice is not intended literally, although as suggested above for Ps. 51.21 the verse may have been given a figurative interpretation.

Psalm 26

This psalm does not directly mention the act of sacrifice, but in v. 8 the psalmist declares his love of the temple as Yahweh's dwelling-place and the place where his glory abides (*m^{e}qôm miškan k^{e}bôd^{e}kā*). Verses 6-7 refer to certain ritual acts performed at the altar of burnt offerings (*mizbēaḥ*) in the temple precincts. The psalmist, who is primarily concerned with his ritual cleansing and his intention to express his thanks to God, does not give a full description of these rites but leaves the central action to be taken for granted. What is described in v. 6 is a ritual ablution perhaps comparable with that commanded to be performed by Aaron and his sons (that is, the priests) before their ministrations at the altar (Exod. 30.17-21; cf. Ps. 73.13 where the same phrase is used in a figurative sense), the purpose of which is to be cleansed from defilement—here, from contact with evildoers (vv. 4-5). In the same verse (v. 6) the circumambulation of the altar, a rite not specifically prescribed in the ritual laws of the Old Testament, may be compared with the description in Ps. 118.27b, which, though its meaning is not entirely clear (see below), certainly refers to a procession connected with the altar.

Thus the most natural interpretation of Ps. 26.6 is that it refers to preparations for the performance of an animal sacrifice (*zebaḥ* or *š^{e}lāmîm*, regularly offered in thanksgiving) which will be carried out on the altar, although the text only hints at this. Verse 7 refers to the singing of a song of thanksgiving (*tôdâ*) in which Yahweh's marvellous deeds will be recounted. As has been seen above, *tôdâ* eventually acquired the meaning of a song sung as a *substitute* for a thanksgiving sacrifice; but in the worship of the temple and before the altar such a song was used as an accompaniment to the sacrifice, declaring its purpose.[9] The mention of the altar makes it clear that a sacrifice is implied here. To interpret these two verses as referring to non-sacrificial worship would be unnatural, unless the word *mizbēaḥ*, 'altar', itself were 'spiritualized'—a surmise for which there is no evidence in the Old Testament.

Psalm 27

This psalm has been supposed by a number of commentators to be composite: vv. 1-6 are an individual's prayer in which he expresses confidence in God's help and protection; but v. 7 has been thought to be the beginning of a separate lamentation, which also moves to a note of confidence at the end. However this may be, we are concerned here only

9. See *TDOT*, V, pp. 436-37 and the biblical references there.

with vv. 1-6, in which the psalmist states that his one desire is to find shelter in Yahweh's presence in the temple. It has been suggested that the central couplet of the overlong v. 4, in which the psalmist requests that he may live in Yahweh's house all the days of his life (*šibtî b^{e}bêt-yhwh kol-y^{e}mê ḥayyay*), is an addition to the text modelled on Ps. 23.6b, *w^{e}šabtî b^{e}bêt yhwh l^{e}ʾōrek yāmîm*. There is also an affinity with Ps. 26.8, where the psalmist, having stated his intention to sing a song of thanksgiving (v. 7), declares his love for the temple, Yahweh's dwelling-place. It may be this common theme that decided the juxtaposition of these two psalms.

In Ps. 27.6b the psalmist states his intention to offer 'sacrifices of jubilation' (*zib^{e}ḥê t^{e}rûʿâ*), probably the equivalent of *zib^{e}ḥê tôdâ*, and to sing in praise of Yahweh. In the context this almost certainly referred to a *sacrifice* of thanksgiving, a view that perhaps finds confirmation in v. 4b, where the verb *biqqēr* (*ûl^{e}baqqēr b^{e}hêkālô*) may denote seeking for an omen in connection with the offering of a sacrifice (cf. Mowinckel[10] and Kraus). However, it has been suggested that, although v. 6 almost certainly originally referred to a sacrifice, *zib^{e}hê t^{e}rûʿâ* could have been interpreted in terms of a *song* of thanksgiving.

Psalms 42–43

This double psalm, though it does not specifically mention sacrifice, clearly alludes to it in 42.5 and 43.4. Here again there is expressed a great longing on the part of the psalmist to participate once again in the temple rites, which he is evidently unable to do. In 42.5 he sadly recalls the past, when he was one of the crowd keeping festival (*hāmôn ḥôgēg*) with ritual shouts (*rinnâ*) of thanksgiving (*tôdâ*), going in procession to the temple. In 43.4 he begs to be allowed once more to participate in those rites: to go to the altar and to join in a song of praise accompanied by the lyre (*kinnôr*). Although this is the lament of an isolated individual, he is looking forward not to a private service of prayer and thanksgiving but to public festival worship involving the altar (*mizbēaḥ*), which in the context can only mean the altar of burnt offerings standing in the temple court before the temple itself. This psalm could only have been used in non-cultic worship if there had been a complete spiritualization of the word 'altar'.[11]

10. *Psalmenstudien*, I, p. 146.

11. See N.E. Wagner, 'רִנָּה in the Psalter', *VT* 10 (1960), pp. 435-41 on the cultic use of *rinnâ*.

Psalm 54

In v. 8 of this psalm the psalmist vows to sacrifice (*ʾezbeḥâ*) to God in the form of a voluntary offering (*nedābâ*). It was suggested by Briggs that this verse is a gloss and not part of the original psalm, on the grounds that it interrupts the connection between vv. 7 and 9. However this may be, it is probable that the word *nedābâ*, 'vow, gift', in this context refers to animal sacrifice. It is a word that can simply denote spontaneity or willingness (Hos. 14.5; Ps. 110.3), but it is most frequently used of animal sacrifice offered voluntarily by an individual on a special occasion, often as the fulfilment of a vow (see for example Lev. 7.16; 22.18; Deut. 23.24). The circumstances of Ps. 54.8 appear to fit this sense: the verb employed is *zābaḥ*; the psalmist promises to make his sacrifice as a *nedābâ* but also to thank Yahweh for delivering him from his trouble, using the phrase 'I will give thanks to your name...for it is good', a phrase comparable with that used on other similar occasions (Pss. 52.11; 107.1; 118.1).

This interpretation has been almost unanimously accepted by the commentators. However, Briggs drew attention to the fact that there is one Old Testament text in which the word *nedābâ* is used to denote the non-sacrificial offering of prayer rather than animal, or even vegetable, sacrifice, or indeed any tangible offering: Ps. 119.108. There the psalmist requests God to accept his *nidebôt pî*, 'the offerings of my mouth'; and there is no hint of their being accompanied by a ritual act. Thus although the original meaning of Ps. 54.8 is of an animal sacrifice, the unique case of Ps. 119.108 may suggest that that verse could have been similarly interpreted—but only if the verb *zābaḥ* were also susceptible of a spiritualized interpretation.

Psalm 66

This psalm consists of two, possibly three, parts: a hymn (vv. 1-7) is followed by a communal thanksgiving (vv. 8-12); vv. 13-20, however, are an individual thanksgiving, in which the psalmist calls on others (v. 16) to listen to his account of God's gracious acceptance of his prayers, and so implicitly invites them to share in his joy. There is perhaps a further distinction to be made between vv. 13-15 and vv. 16-19 (20).

Verses 13-15 depict a situation in which the psalmist is preparing to fulfil an earlier vow, made when he was in trouble, to offer thanksgiving sacrifices when Yahweh should had intervened on his behalf. The emphatic reference to the sacrifice of animals in vv. 13-15, in which the psalmist speaks of offering burnt sacrifices (*ʿôlôt*) of fat beasts (*mēḥîm*), rams (*ʾēlîm*), oxen (*bāqār*) and goats (*ʿattûdîm*) is unmistakable and hardly capable of a spiritualizing interpretation; such detailed listing is a rarity in the Psalter (Barnes). In view of the great number of animals involved it would seem either that the worshipper was an exceptionally wealthy or influential individual (it has been suggested that he was a king), or that he is here speaking of his part in a large-scale communal thanksgiving festival.[12]

Verses 16-20, on the other hand, make no further mention of animal sacrifice, but only of the psalmist's *prayer*. This clearly refers to his vow, which God has accepted because it was offered in sincerity and with a pure heart (v. 18). This was evidently a private experience which the worshipper now describes to others. It was, then, this vow to which God had reacted. The sacrifices that the worshipper is now about to offer are not the cause of this favourable reaction, but are thanksgiving sacrifices offered in fulfilment of the vow. There is thus no contradiction between the verses that refer to sacrifice and the final verses. Nevertheless the switch from the section on sacrifice to that on prayer is somewhat surprising, although there is no reason to suspect that vv. 16-20 are a later addition to the psalm by a redactor who wished to make the point that prayer is more effective than animal sacrifice. It must be concluded that this is a psalm in which no attempt has been made to modify the evident approval of the practice of animal sacrifice.

Psalm 107

On the structure of this psalm see Chapter 2 above and also Beyerlin.[13] Of the four refrains (vv. 8, 15, 21-22, 31), in which various groups of people who have successfully appealed to Yahweh in their distress are urged to give thanks to him at the thanksgiving festival, only vv. 21-22 add an admonition to 'offer sacrifices of thanksgiving' (*wᵉyizbᵉḥû zibᵉḥê tôdâ*, v. 22) as well as to give a public oral testimony to God's action in delivering them. It is not clear why the reference to sacrifice occurs only at this point in the psalm; but there can be no doubt that the reference to

12. See J.M. O'Brien, '"Because God Heard My Voice": The Individual Thanksgiving Psalm and Vow-Fulfilment', in K.G. Hoglund *et al.* (eds.), *The Listening Heart: Essays in Wisdom and the Psalms in Honor of Roland E. Murphy, O. Carm* (JSOTSup, 58; Sheffield: JSOT Press, 1987), pp. 281-98.

13. *Werden und Wesen des 107. Psalms.*

sacrificial offerings was literally intended. Whether or not a spiritualization of the reference was possible, there has once again been no editorial attempt to encourage this by textual alteration.

Psalm 116

This psalm is essentially an individual thanksgiving, but its structure is not clear, and there are some strange transitions of thought. Gunkel commented[14] that the author was 'certainly no great independent poet'. One of the signs of confusion is that v. 14 is exactly repeated in v. 18, though there is no reason to suppose that the verse was intended to function as a refrain. Several commentators have noted that the author has incorporated earlier material into his work in which reference is made to concepts and practices that were now obsolete. The main theme of the psalm, however, is a familiar one: the psalmist states his intention of publicly fulfilling an earlier vow to Yahweh in thanksgiving for his deliverance from imminent death.

Verse 13a is the most obvious example of a reference to an old ritual. The psalmist states 'I will lift up the cup of salvation (*kôs yᵉšûʿôt ʾeśśāʾ*) and call on the name of Yahweh'. No agreement has been reached about this cup ritual. It has been variously interpreted as a drink offering or libation or as the enactment of an 'ordeal' (cf. Num. 5.23-31). Phoenician and other pagan parallels have been adduced, but such a ritual seems to have been otherwise unknown in Israel, at least in historical times; at all events there is no other passage in the Old Testament that refers to it. All that can be said is that it appears to have signified the worshipper's freeing from his 'bonds', perhaps the bonds of his sin. There is reason to believe, in view of the uniqueness of the reference, that the line should be understood in a metaphorical sense. Kraus saw it as a dim reflection of some obsolete practice whose original meaning had been long forgotten.

The figurative interpretation of v. 13a may have influenced that of v. 17, where the psalmist makes the promise 'To you will I sacrifice a sacrifice of thanksgiving and call upon the name of Yahweh' (*lᵉkā ʾezbaḥ zebaḥ tôdâ ûbᵉšēm yhwh ʾeqrāʾ*). Kraus suggested that the verb *zābaḥ* and the noun *zebaḥ* here (and so presumably elsewhere in the Psalms) ought perhaps to be understood in a spiritualizing sense: 'It is a question whether the ancient sacrificial practice is still preserved here, or

14. *Die Psalmen*, p. 502.

whether the *tôdâ* of the song of thanksgiving comprises in itself all that was in later times signified by "thanksgiving sacrifice".' This dilution of the meaning of *zbḥ*, however, remains uncertain; if Kraus's view is correct it would have been unnecessary for a redactor to attempt to 'correct' the text.

Psalm 118

Although this psalm mentions the altar of sacrifice in the temple court with its 'horns' as the centre of ritual activity (v. 27), it has been maintained by some scholars that the psalm makes no allusion at all to animal sacrifice. There are many textual problems here. The psalm is probably composite, and various voices are heard in it. Kraus is probably right in classifying it as a thanksgiving festival liturgy, part of which took place before the temple gates and was concerned with a request to enter the temple (cf. Pss. 15 and 24).

The question whether animal sacrifice is envisaged here depends on the interpretation of v. 27bc, *ʾisrû-ḥag bāʿᵃbōtîm*, the meaning of which is greatly disputed. A literal rendering would be 'bind the festival with cords' (though *ʿᵃbōtîm* can also mean 'branches' or 'foliage', as, for instance, in Ezek. 19.11). Older modern translations and some commentators (such as Schmidt) understood *ḥag* here as denoting the sacrificial victim; but the word never has this meaning. Anderson and Allen suggested that the verb *ʾāsar* here means 'begin', so that *ʾisrû-ḥag* would signify 'Begin the festival!'; but this sense of *ʾāsar* is found only in the expression 'begin (i.e. join) battle' (1 Kgs 20.14; 2 Chron. 13.3).

The festival in question is probably the Feast of Tabernacles,[15] when according to the Mishnah[16] palm and myrtle branches and branches of other trees were brought to the temple and carried in procession round the altar.[17] This was of course followed by the sacrifice of animals on the altar (cf. Meysing[18]).

Meysing introduced a further consideration into the discussion with a new interpretation of *wayyāʾēr* in v. 27a. This is the *hiphil* of *ʾôr*, whose most frequent connotations are 'give light', 'enlighten', and the line *ʾēl*

15. J.J. Petuchowski, '"Hoshi'ah na" in Psalm cxviii—A Prayer for Rain', *VT* 5 (1955), pp. 266-71.

16. *Suk.* 3.8, 12; 4.4, 5.

17. Cf. Ps. 26.6 and see Josephus, *Ant.* 3.10.4.

18. J. Meysing, 'A Text-Reconstruction of Ps. cxvii (cxviii) 27', *VT* 10 (1960), pp. 130-37.

yhwh wayyāʾēr lānû has usually been rendered by 'Yahweh is God, and he has given us light.' Meysing took the verb in the less frequent sense of 'kindle, set light to' (cf. Mal. 1.10, where the phrase *wᵉlōʾ-tāʾîrû mizbᵉḥî ḥinnām*, addressed to the unworthy priests, may mean 'and you shall not kindle [a fire] on my altar to no purpose').[19] In the same verse *ʿᵃbōtîm* could refer to the branches or twigs disposed by the worshippers around the altar which were to be used to make the fire for the sacrifice.

Whether Meysing's interpretation of the verse is correct in all its details or not (it also involves the emendation of *ʾisrû* to *ʿᵃśû*, so that *ʿᵃśû ḥag* would mean 'perform the feast'), there is good reason to understand Ps. 118.27 as a command by the officiating priest to the worshippers to kindle the wood for the burnt offering. Only after the destruction of the temple in 70 CE might it have been possible to reinterpret v. 27 in terms of a non-sacrificial observance of the Feast of Tabernacles.

Conclusion

The above survey of references and possible references to animal sacrifice in the Psalter has been somewhat inconclusive in the sense that much depends on the plausibility of the theory that some sacrificial terms—specifically, the verb *zābaḥ* and the noun *zebaḥ*—lost their original meaning of the slaughtering of animals and came to denote other, non-sacrificial, modes of worship, notably the *song* of thanksgiving, which could be offered either publicly or privately. It was concluded that there is no evidence for this development either in the Old Testament text or, as absence of such a development, in postbiblical Hebrew. This is not surprising: these words—together with *mizbēaḥ*—might be supposed to have been studiously avoided by those to whom sacrificial worship was abhorrent or distasteful.

It is appropriate to enquire, then, what evidence is to be found concerning the interpretations placed by those who rejected animal sacrifice on the psalms in question. Evidence of redactional 'correction' is sparse, though this may have occurred in at least one case (Ps. 40). But the fact that in the majority of cases texts which express strong approval of sacrifice were incorporated into the final edition of the Psalter without modification is surprising. It is clear that no attempt was made to undertake a systematic redaction of the Psalter from an anti-sacrificial point of

19. So H. Graf Reventlow, *Die Propheten Haggai, Sacharja und Maleachi* (ATD, 25.2; Göttingen: Vandenhoeck & Ruprecht, 1993), pp. 138-41.

view. It is true, as has been pointed out above, that some of the relevant psalms are ambiguous in this respect and could have been silently reinterpreted in terms of private worship, but others (such as Pss. 26; 51; 66; 118) are so explicit in their references that this would have presented considerable difficulties. Thus while the Psalter does testify to the work of redactors of individual psalms who made 'corrections' to offending passages, it is clear that there was no systematic activity of this kind in the final redaction of the book.

CONCLUSION

The purpose of this investigation has been to consider the theory that the aim of those who carried out the final redaction of the Psalter was to produce a 'book' (as distinct from a mere collection of unrelated items) that could be read through from beginning to end as a coherent work of piety or instruction: a book whose various parts (that is, the 150 individual psalms) were ordered in such a way as to present a single comprehensive message.

After a survey of earlier studies (Chapter 1), the wisdom and Torah material in the Psalter was studied in order to test the view, expressed by a number of recent scholars, that the placing of this material had been chosen by the final redactor or redactors in order to give the whole Psalter a distinctive theological tone. But since it seems to me that the mere placing of certain wisdom psalms would have been insufficient to achieve that purpose, the possibility was examined (Chapter 2) that some other psalms which originally lacked any wisdom or Torah features might have been adapted through textual additions to strengthen the undertaking. Two other themes, prominent in the Psalms, were then chosen that might have been thought by readers to require serious modification: kingship and ritual sacrifice—themes that would have come to be seen by many as irrelevant or distasteful (Chapters 3 and 4).

It was concluded that there was no comprehensive editing of the Psalter along any of the lines suggested above. However, this does not necessarily mean that the Psalter in its final form was *not* used as a book to be read for purposes of private edification from an early date. This may well have been the case: there is no clear information on the point, though the fact that the Psalms have been used for such purposes throughout subsequent history may suggest that it was. The worship of Israel undoubtedly underwent great changes during the post-exilic period, even during the period of the Second Temple, though the details of the change elude scholars.

But while a small number of psalms have been shown to have been added to the collection or textually adapted for such purposes, this was carried out only sporadically. There is no evidence that there was a systematic and purposeful redaction of the whole Psalter in any of the suggested ways. Although it is obvious that obsolete or distasteful features of the Psalms have in fact been consistently reinterpreted by readers symbolically, there is no evidence of consistent *textual* manipulation serving such a purpose. The reinterpretations must have been 'silent', as each reader—or, later, church or synagogue tradition—struggled to make the Psalter relevant to later generations.

Unfortunately there is no direct evidence (except Ps. 72.20), internal or external, about the process by which the Psalter received its shape. All hypotheses about this basic question are purely speculative, based on inferences drawn from textual data that can be, and often have been, interpreted in quite different ways by different scholars (so Murphy). All that can be said with reasonable certainty about the process is that it was extremely complex, took place over a considerable time, and was influenced at its various stages by different editorial policies (Millard).

There is no lack of evidence to show that particular groups of psalms within the Psalter were formed for different purposes and at different times. Thus most of the superscriptions linking groups of psalms—for instance the two groups of David psalms, the Asaph and Korah psalms and the Songs of Ascents—were no doubt added for different reasons and at different times. This is true, for example, of the different groups of David psalms: the expanded superscriptions that refer to particular incidents of David's life presumably served a different purpose from those attached to other David psalms. The groups of David psalms as they now stand have undoubtedly undergone a complex editing process. Further, no adequate explanation has been found for the identical superscriptions attached to isolated David psalms. The problem is further complicated by the fact that the superscriptions in the LXX by no means correspond exactly to those in the Hebrew text. The superscriptions can in any case account only for the grouping of a proportion of the psalms in the Psalter, and there is no reason to suppose that they were all added at the same stage in the composition of the book.

We also remain in ignorance of the date and the purpose of the division of the Psalter into five Books. This division was already observed in the LXX (second century BCE), but there is no reason why it could not have been made well before that. Wilson claimed that it is not arbitrary but reflects the history of 'purposeful editorial activity within the text of the canonical psalter'.[1] He claimed that Books I–III were arranged in accordance with supposed authorship, whereas in Books IV–V the main organizational technique was the use of 'genre terms' in the superscriptions. Wilson also found evidence of a subsequent attempt to link the Books together by means of 'seams'. The difficulty with such theories—Wilson's is only one of several—is that they paint on a very broad canvas, paying insufficient attention to the contents of most individual psalms, whose apparent randomness of arrangement (for instance the mingling of psalms of praise with psalms of lament) remains a stumbling-block for those who fail to find any consistency or overarching structure or plan to the book. Any theory of a coherent pattern ought surely to provide some explanation of the arrangement of the *whole* collection.

Wisdom and Torah Psalms

A consideration of wisdom and Torah psalms and similar material in the Psalter led to the conclusion that most of the purely wisdom and Torah psalms were not placed in positions that suggest a comprehensive redactional intention, and that the wisdom additions to non-wisdom psalms were made *ad hoc* wherever a need or opportunity presented itself to an individual editor rather than in the interest of a system. Psalm 73, described by McCann as a 'microcosm of theology', may be an exception in so far as its position exactly at the midpoint of the Psalter could be significant and may point to an intention—not, however, fully implemented—at a late stage in the redaction of the book to accentuate the importance of wisdom theology. The inclusion of Psalm 119 in the collection—a psalm whose inordinate length, as well as its contents, marks it out as of exceptional importance—may have been intended to perform a similar function for Torah theology, although it is difficult to see why it has been placed where it has. (Westermann's suggestion that at one stage in the composition of the book this psalm marked the conclusion of the Psalter, which would then have been a work wholly framed by Torah psalms, is purely speculative.)

With regard to Psalm 1, although it would probably be incorrect to call it an 'introduction' to the Psalter intended to motivate the reader to read the whole book through 'hermeneutical spectacles' (as Wilson suggested), it is no doubt true that this psalm was placed in its initial position to instil

1. 'Evidence of Editorial Divisions in the Hebrew Psalter', p. 337.

in the reader the importance of a redactor's conviction, also expressed in Psalm 119, that meditation on the Torah—which does *not* mean meditation on the Psalter—is the indispensable means for the attainment of divine blessing.

Concatenation

One method that has been employed in recent research to demonstrate editorial purpose in the Psalter is the study of concatenations: that is, the linking of adjacent psalms either by theme or verbally by 'catchwords' and repeated identical poetical lines, so forming a series of catenae (cf. Zimmerli and C. Barth[2]). As far as purely verbal links are concerned, there is no doubt that such are to be found between pairs and even small groups of psalms. However, given the large element of constantly repeated common vocabulary in the Psalter and in view of the probability that the psalmists were accustomed to compose by drawing on a common stock of pre-fabricated poetical lines,[3] many if not most of these supposed links can probably be put down to coincidence or are for other reasons devoid of editorial significance. Thematic linking is another matter; but although such pairs and small groups of adjacent psalms are certainly to be found, such evidence of small-scale editorial work does not in any way conduce to the plausibility of a comprehensive theory of a single, purposive redaction of the whole Psalter. Only if it could be shown that every psalm is linked to its immediate neighbours could such a theory be tenable.

From Lament to Praise, from Death to Life

A somewhat different approach to the understanding of the Psalter in its final form has been proposed. This views the book from a broader perspective than other theories, discerning in it a single, though nuanced, progression from one mood to another—or, in other words, a consistent

2. W. Zimmerli, 'Zwillingspsalmen', in J. Schreiner (ed.), *Wort, Lied und Gottesspruch: Beiträge zu Psalmen und Propheten* (Festschrift J. Ziegler; Würzburg: Echter Verlag, 1972), pp. 105-13; C. Barth, 'Concatenatio im Ersten Buch des Psalters', in B. Benzing, O. Böcher and G. Mayer (eds.), *Wort und Wirklichkeit* (Festschrift E.L. Rapp; Meisenheim am Glan, 1976), pp. 30-40.

3. See R.C. Culley, *Oral Formulaic Language in the Biblical Psalms* (Toronto: University of Toronto Press, 1967).

theological progression. The main proponent of this theory is Brueggemann. He begins with the observation that Book I (Pss. 1–41) contains an exceptionally large number of lamentations, while the whole Psalter concludes (in Pss. 146–150 and especially Ps. 150) with psalms of pure praise—a fact that may reasonably be supposed to call for an explanation. For Brueggemann, Psalms 1 and 150 represent the extreme poles of a movement which he describes variously as one 'from obedience to praise', 'from duty to delight', 'from hurt to joy', 'from death to life'. The centrally placed Psalm 73, with its affirmation of trust in God which eventually overcomes doubts, suffering and guilt, he regards as a turning point marking a fundamental change of mood. The Psalter is thus 'bounded by obedience and praise',[4] and is so ordered as to take the readers step by step through the crisis of *ḥesed*, which they have experienced as they wrestled with their various disappointments and trials, to a confident conclusion.

Brueggemann insists that his principal concern is neither with the 'shape' of the Psalter—that is, with the placing of every psalm—nor with 'history' (e.g., in the sense of a historical development in which a positive treatment of the Davidic monarchy was followed by a reminder of the failure of that monarchy, so leading to an emphasis on the absolute sovereignty of God in a period when there was no reigning Israelite king). His concern is synchronic (though he does not use this term): a concern with the Psalter as canon. The Psalter, with all its diversity, presents when interpreted symbolically a fundamentally coherent message which served the needs of the faithful reader.

Although there are problems in the pursuance of this approach—notably with regard to Brueggemann's explanation of the themes of Books III and IV and the fact that hymns occur throughout the Psalter and not only at the end—it may well be that with its more modest aims it is more plausible in its argument for a comprehensive editorial policy than more meticulous attempts to account for every detail in the structuring of the Psalter.

Royal Psalms and Psalms Referring to Ritual Sacrifice

The survey of these psalms was made partly as a reminder that in the post-exilic period which saw the final redaction of the Psalter, and possibly earlier, there were other perceived needs for theological 'corrections'

4. This is the title of his article in *JSOT* 50 (1991).

of older psalms than their interpretation in terms of the theologies of Torah and wisdom. In particular, it was necessary to come to terms with the loss of monarchy, and this was, in some circles, achieved by reading the royal psalms eschatologically and messianically; and with an antipathy towards ritual sacrifice (or simply a feeling that it was irrelevant and unnecessary) that also needed to be catered for. Reinterpretation of the Psalms thus needed to take place on more than one level: eschatology and Torah theology, for example, were not characteristic of the same religious group.

A second purpose of the survey of these two kinds of psalm was to discover how far, if at all, there are indications in the text of *redactional* attempts to modify or reinterpret the psalms' original meaning. As with the wisdom and Torah material, it was concluded that there is only slight evidence of this. In the case of the royal psalms this lack of such alterations to the text is probably due to the fact that they frequently speak of the king in grandiose and even mysterious terms that could easily be interpreted messianically without any need for textual 'corrections'. In the case of those psalms that refer with approval to ritual sacrifice, however, a comparable conclusion is possible only if the term *zebaḥ*, 'sacrifice', had undergone a radical change of meaning—a view for which there is no certain evidence. In some of these psalms the references to animal sacrifice are so specific and approving of the practice that they might seem certain to have required reinterpretation if they were to be acceptable to one group of readers; but even here no such modification is perceptible in the text.

There remains the question of significant placement of these types of psalm. Wilson's observation that royal psalms occur at what he called the 'seams' of the Psalter (Ps. 2 at the beginning of Book I and Pss. 72 and 89 at the end of Books II and III respectively) must be taken into account. This may point to a redactional emphasis on the theme of the fate of kingship; but, as Wilson himself pointed out, it may equally be an indication of the importance of the messianic hope, though this device is not carried through into Books IV and V. In any case it cannot be maintained that kingship is an all-pervading topic even in Books I–III, while the superscriptions to some at least of the psalms in Books I and II have no eschatological implications.

In conclusion, it is not possible to give a confident answer to the question whether the final redaction of the Psalter was undertaken in order to make it into a single, coherent book to be read privately from beginning to end by devout persons for their instruction or as an aid to their devotion. According to Millard there is no evidence that it was so used in Judaism. That it was so used in the worship of some kind of 'cultic' assembly is improbable, since nothing is known of such a practice, and the Psalter is too long for such use.

On the other hand, there is nothing intrinsically improbable in the notion of private consecutive reading of the Psalms: they have been so used, if not by Jews, certainly by Christians for many centuries in addition to their use in public and collegial worship. One reason why they have been read in this way—that is, in the order in which they now occur in the Psalter—is that the varying moods that they express may be said to reflect the whole life and experience of the worshippers with their moods of exaltation and depression, but never of despair: trust in God is never absent. In their unexpected changes of mood the psalms also reflect the irregularities and uncertainties of the life of faith. The first psalm and the final psalms, however, are fixed boundaries within which the life of faith moves.

From an early period—long before the final redaction—the psalms must already have been 'silently' reinterpreted by the faithful, by means of a partly unconscious symbolic exegesis, and in various ways in accordance with different spiritual convictions and needs. There is evidence that in a few instances such reinterpretation was effected in the form of textual additions; but for the most part such reinterpretation was achieved, as it is today, by 'silent' means. There is no evidence of the thorough and systematic changes that would have been necessary if the Psalter were to become the expression of a single theology. The stages by which it took its present shape lie mainly beyond our knowing.

BIBLIOGRAPHY

Albertz, R., *A History of Israelite Religion in the Old Testament Period*, II (London: SCM Press, 1994; ET of *Religionsgeschichte Israels in alttestamentlicher Zeit*, II [Göttingen: Vandenhoeck & Ruprecht, 1992]).

Alter, R., 'Psalms', in R. Alter and F. Kermode (eds.), *The Literary Guide to the Bible* (London: Collins, 1987), pp. 244-62.

Anderson, G.W. ' "Sicut Cervus": Evidence in the Psalter of Private Devotion in Ancient Israel', *VT* 30 (1980), pp. 388-97.

Auffret, P., *The Literary Structure of Psalm 2* (JSOTSup, 3; Sheffield: JSOT Press, 1977).

Barth, C., 'Concatenatio im Ersten Buch des Psalters', in B. Benzing, O. Böcher and G. Mayer (eds.), *Wort und Wirklichkeit* (Festschrift E.L. Rapp; Meisenheim am Glan, 1976), pp. 30-40.

Begrich, J., 'Das priesterliche Heilsorakel', *ZAW* 52 (1934), pp. 81-92.

Bennett, R.A., 'Wisdom Motifs in Psalm 14 = 53 -*nābāl* and *ʿesāh*', *BASOR* 220 (1975), pp. 15-21.

Beyerlin, W., *Werden und Wesen des 107. Psalms* (BZAW, 153; Berlin: de Gruyter, 1979).

Brueggemann, W., 'Bounded by Obedience and Praise: The Psalms as Canon', *JSOT* 50 (1991), pp. 63-92.

—'Response to James L. Mays, "The Question of Context" ', in McCann (ed.), *Shape and Shaping*, pp. 29-41.

—*The Psalms and the Life of Faith* (Minneapolis: Fortress Press, 1995).

Carroll, R.P., 'Psalm lxxviii: Vestiges of a Tribal Polemic', *VT* 21 (1971), pp. 133-50.

Childs, B.S., *Introduction to the Old Testament as Scripture* (London: SCM Press, 1979), pp. 508-23.

Crenshaw, J.L., 'Wisdom', in J.H. Hayes (ed.), *Old Testament Form Criticism* (San Antonio: Trinity University Press, 1974), pp. 225-64.

Culley, R.C., *Oral Formulaic Language in the Biblical Psalms* (Toronto: University of Toronto Press, 1967).

Dalglish, E.R., *Psalm Fifty-One in the Light of Ancient Near Eastern Patternism* (Leiden: Brill, 1962).

Engnell, I., 'The Book of Psalms', in J.T. Willis and H. Ringgren (eds.), *Critical Essays on the Old Testament* (London: SPCK, 1970), pp. 68-122.

Golka, F.W., 'Die israelitische Weisheitsschule oder "des Kaisers neue Kleider" ', *VT* 33 (1983), pp. 257-71.

Grabbe, L.L., *Judaism from Cyrus to Hadrian*, I (Minneapolis: Fortress Press, 1992; London: SCM Press, 1994).

Gunkel, H., *Einleitung in die Psalmen. Die Gattungen der religiösen Lyrik Israels, zu Ende geführt von Joachim Begrich* (Göttingen: Vandenhoeck & Ruprecht, 1933).

Haran, M., 'The Uses of Incense in the Ancient Israelite Ritual', *VT* 10 (1960), pp. 113-29.

Howard, D.M., Jr, 'Editorial Activity in the Psalter: A State-of-the Field Survey', in McCann (ed.), *Shape and Shaping*, pp. 52-70.
Jacquet, L., *Les Psaumes et le coeur de l'homme*, I (Gembloux: Duculot, 1975).
Jansen, H.L., *Die spätjüdische Psalmendichtung* (SNVAO, 3; Oslo, 1937).
Koole, J.L., 'Quelques remarques sur le Psaume 139', in W.C. van Unnik and A.S. van der Woude (eds.), *Studia Biblica T.C. Vriezen ...Dedicata* (Wageningen: Veenman & Zonen, 1966), pp. 176-80.
Kraus, H.-J., *Psalmen*, I (BKAT, 15; Neukirchen–Vluyn: Neukirchener Verlag, 1961).
Kruse, H., 'Psalm cxxxii and the Royal Zion Festival', *VT* 33 (1983), pp. 279-97.
Kuntz, J.K., 'The Retribution Motif in Psalmic Wisdom', *ZAW* 89 (1977), pp. 223-33.
Lang, B., 'Schule und Unterricht im alten Israel', in M. Gilbert (ed.), *La Sagesse de l'Ancien Testament* (BETL, 51; Gembloux: Duculot; Leuven: Leuven University Press, 1979), pp. 186-201.
Lescow, T., 'Textübergreifende Exegese: Zur Lesung von Ps 24–26', *ZAW* 107 (1955), pp. 65-79.
Liedke, G. and C. Petersen, '*tōrā* Weisung', *THAT*, II, pp. 1032–43.
Lindars, B., 'Torah in Deuteronomy', in P.R. Ackroyd and B. Lindars (eds.), *Words and Meanings: Essays Presented to David Winton Thomas* (Cambridge: Cambridge University Press, 1968), pp. 117-36.
Lipiński, E., 'Macarismes et psaumes de congratulation', *RB* 75 (1968), pp. 330-39.
Marx, A., *Les offrandes végétales dans l'Ancien Testament* (VTSup, 57; Leiden: Brill, 1994).
Mays, J.L., 'The Place of the Torah-Psalms in the Psalter', *JBL* 106 (1987), pp. 3-12.
—'The Question of Context in Psalm Interpretation', in McCann (ed.), *Shape and Shaping*, pp. 14-20.
McCann, J.C., Jr, 'Psalm 73: A Microcosm of Old Testament Theology', in K.G. Hoglund *et al.* (eds.), *The Listening Heart: Essays in Wisdom and the Psalms in Honor of Roland E. Murphy, O. Carm* (JSOTSup, 58; Sheffield: JSOT Press, 1987), pp. 247-57.
—'The Psalms as Instruction', *Int* 46 (1992), pp. 117-28.
—'Books I–III and the Editorial Purpose of the Hebrew Psalter', in *idem* (ed.), *Shape and Shaping*, pp. 93-107.
McCann, J.C., Jr (ed.), *The Shape and Shaping of the Psalter* (JSOTSup, 159; Sheffield: JSOT Press, 1993).
Meer, W. van der, 'Psalm 110: A Psalm of Rehabilitation?', in W. van der Meer and J.C. de Moor (eds.), *The Structural Analysis of Biblical and Canaanite Poetry* (JSOTSup, 74; Sheffield: JSOT Press, 1988), pp. 207-34.
Meysing, J., 'A Text-Reconstruction of Ps. cxvii (cxviii) 27', *VT* 10 (1960), pp. 130-37.
Millard, M., *Die Komposition des Psalters*, (Forschungen zum Alten Testament, 9; Tübingen: Mohr, 1994).
Miller, P.D., Jr, 'Psalm 127—The House that Yahweh Builds', *JSOT* 22 (1982), pp. 119-32.
—'The Beginning of the Psalter', in McCann (ed.), *Shape and Shaping*, pp. 83-92.
Mowinckel, S., *Psalmenstudien*. I. *Åwän und die individuellen Klagepsalmen* (ANVAO hist.-fil. kl. 1921, 4); reprinted in *Psalmenstudien*, I (Amsterdam: P. Schiffers, 1961).
—*Psalmenstudien:* VI. *Die Psalmdichter* (ANVAO hist.-fil. kl. no. 1, 1924); reprinted in *Psalmenstudien*, II (Amsterdam: P. Schiffers, 1961).
—*Offersang og Sangoffer* (Oslo: Aschehoug, 1951; ET with revisions, *The Psalms in Israel's Worship* [Oxford: Basil Blackwell, 1962]).

—'Psalms and Wisdom', in M. Noth and D.W. Thomas (eds.), *Wisdom in Israel and the Ancient Near East* (VTSup, 3; Leiden: Brill, 1955), pp. 205-24.

Murphy, R.E., 'A Consideration of the Classification "Wisdom Psalms" ', in J.A. Emerton *et al.* (eds.), *Congress Volume, Bonn 1962* (VTSup, 9; Leiden: Brill, 1963), pp. 156-67.

—'Reflections on Contextual Interpretation of the Psalms', in McCann (ed.), *Shape and Shaping*, pp. 21-28.

Nielsen, E., 'Psalm 73: Scandinavian Contributions', in A.G. Auld (ed.), *Understanding Poets and Prophets. Essays in Honour of George Wishart Anderson* (JSOTSup, 152; Sheffield: JSOT Press, 1993), pp. 273-83.

O'Brien, J.M., ' "Because God Heard My Voice": The Individual Thanksgiving Psalm and Vow-Fulfilment', in K.G. Hoglund *et al.* (eds.), *The Listening Heart: Essays in Wisdom and the Psalms in Honor of Roland E. Murphy, O. Carm.* (JSOTSup, 58; Sheffield: JSOT Press), pp. 281-98.

Petuchowski, J.J., ' "Hoshiʿah na" in Psalm cxviii 25,—A Prayer for Rain', *VT* 5 (1955), pp. 266-71.

Ploeg, J.P.M. van der, 'Le sens et un problème textuel du Ps lxxxix', in A. Caquot and M. Delcor (eds.), *Mélanges bibliques en l'honneur de M. Henri Cazelles* (AOAT 212; Kevelaer: Butzon & Bercker; Neukirchen–Vluyn: Neukirchener Verlag, 1981), pp. 471-81.

von Rad, G., *Weisheit in Israel* (Neukirchen–Vluyn: Neukirchener Verlag, 1970; ET *Wisdom in Israel* [London: SCM Press, 1972]).

—'Der 90. Psalm', in *Gottes Wirken in Israel. Vorträge zum Alten Testament* (Neukirchen–Vluyn: Neukirchener Verlag, 1976), pp. 268-83.

Reindl, J., 'Weisheitliche Bearbeitung von Psalmen. Ein Beitrag zum Verständnis der Sammlung des Psalters', in J.A. Emerton (ed.), *Congress Volume, Vienna 1980* (VTSup, 32; Leiden: Brill, 1981), pp. 333-54.

Reventlow, H. Graf, *Die Propheten Haggai, Sacharja und Maleachi* (ATD, 25.2; Göttingen: Vandenhoeck & Ruprecht, 1993).

Ridderbos, N.H., 'The Structure of Psalm xl', in P.A.H. De Boer (ed.), כה *1940–1965* (OTS, 14; Leiden: Brill, 1965), pp. 296-304.

Ruppert, L., 'Psalm 25 und die Grenze kultorientierter Psalmenexegese', *ZAW* 84 (1972), pp. 576-82.

Smith, M.S., 'The Psalms as a Book for Pilgrims', *Int* 46 (1992), pp. 156-66.

Steck, O.H, 'Bemerkungen zur thematischen Einheit von Psalm 19,2-7', in R. Albertz *et al.* (eds.), *Werden und Wirken des Alten Testaments. Festschrift für Claus Westermann zum 70. Geburtstag* (Göttingen: Vandenhoeck & Ruprecht; Neukirchen–Vluyn: Neukirchener Verlag, 1980), pp. 318-24.

—'Beobachtungen zu Psalm 8', in *idem*, *Wahrnehmungen Gottes im Alten Testament* (TBAT, 70; Munich: Chr. Kaiser Verlag, 1982), pp. 221-31.

Tournay, R.J., 'Le Psaume lxxiii: relectures et interprétation', *RB* 92 (1985), pp. 187-99.

Vesco, J.-L., 'Le psaume 18, lecture davidique', *RB* 94 (1987), pp. 5-62.

Wagner, N.E., 'רִנָּה in the Psalter', *VT* 10 (1960), pp. 435-41.

Wagner, S., 'Zur Theologie des Psalms cxxxix', in J.A. Emerton (ed.), *Congress Volume, Göttingen* (VTSup, 29; Leiden: Brill, 1978), pp. 357-76.

Westermann, C., 'Zur Sammlung des Psalters', *Theologia Viatorum* 8 (1962), pp. 278-84 = *Forschung am Alten Testament* (TBAT, 24; Munich: Chr. Kaiser Verlag, 1964), pp. 336-43.

Whybray, R.N., 'Wisdom Psalms', in J. Day, R.P. Gordon and H.G.M. Williamson (eds.), *Wisdom in Ancient Israel: Essays in Honour of J.A. Emerton* (Cambridge: Cambridge University Press, 1995), pp. 152-60.

Willis, J.T., 'Psalm 1—An Entity', *ZAW* 91 (1979), pp. 381-401.

—'A Cry of Defiance—Psalm 2', *JSOT* 47 (1990), pp. 33-50.

Wilson, G.H., 'Evidence of Editorial Divisions in the Hebrew Psalter', *VT* 34 (1984), pp. 337-52.

—*The Editing of the Hebrew Psalter* (SBLDS, 76; Chico, CA: Scholars Press, 1985).

—'The Use of Royal Psalms at the "Seams" of the Hebrew Psalter', *JSOT* 35 (1986), pp. 85-94.

—'The Shape of the Book of Psalms', *Int* 46 (1992), pp. 129-42.

—'A Consideration of Editorial Linkage in the Book of Psalms', in McCann (ed.), *Shape and Shaping*, pp. 72-82.

—'Understanding the Purposeful Arrangement of Psalms in the Psalter: Pitfalls and Promise', in McCann (ed.), *Shape and Shaping*, pp. 42-51.

Würthwein, E., 'Erwägungen zu Psalm cxxxix', *VT* 7 (1957), pp. 165-82.

Zimmerli, W., 'Zwillingspsalmen', in J. Schreiner (ed.), *Wort, Lied und Gottesspruch: Beiträge zu Psalmen und Propheten* (Festschrift J. Ziegler; Würzburg: Echter Verlag, 1972), pp. 105-13.

INDEXES

INDEX OF REFERENCES

OLD TESTAMENT

Genesis
1–3 45, 60
14 95

Exodus
24.8 104
29.41 108
30.17-21 110

Leviticus
1.3-4 43
2.1 108
2.15 108
7.16 112
22.18 112

Numbers
5.23-31 114

Deuteronomy
4.2 69
11.1 69
17.18-19 39, 40
17.19-20 102
23.24 112
28 80
31.9-11 40
33.19 109

Joshua
1.7-8 39
1.7 39
1.8 39, 40

1 Samuel
10.5 65
15.22 100, 103
16.16 65

2 Samuel
7.11-16 91
15–19 95
21.17 98
22 50

1 Kings
20.14 115

2 Kings
3.15 65
16.15 108

1 Chronicles
25.8 16

2 Chronicles
13.3 115
35.10 108
35.16 108

Job
7.7 63
7.19 72
10.6 72
10.8-12 73
10.14 72
10.20 72
11.6 45
12.8-9 45
13.17 45
14.5-12 67
14.16 72
15.17 45
22.2 61
28.28 58
31.4 72
32.6-11 45
34.22 72
36.2-3 45
38.4 45
38.18 45

Psalms
1–119 18
1–41 34, 122
1 12, 17-19, 21, 22, 24, 25, 27, 28, 31-33, 36, 38, 40, 41, 47, 48, 50, 56, 60, 62, 69, 73, 74, 78-81, 84, 85, 120
1.1 38, 69, 79, 80
1.2 19, 38-40, 47, 49, 58, 64, 69
1.3 39, 54
1.4-5 69

1.6 79
1.40-41 49
2–41 80
2 25-28, 33, 78-81, 88, 89, 92, 99, 123
2.2 89
2.6 89
2.7 89, 96
2.8 89
2.10-12 79
2.10-11 80
2.12 79, 80
3–89 20, 22
3 34
4 109
4.2-3 109
4.5 109
4.6 101, 109
7–9 48
7 34
7.6 48
8 36, 58, 60, 61, 73
8.2 60
8.3-9 60
8.3 60
8.4-5 60
8.5 58
8.6 60
10.8-9 56
10.44-45 56
10.45 56
11.7 96
14 61, 73
14.1 61
14.2 61
14.4 61
14.5 61
14.6 61
14.7 61
15 30, 43, 115
17–18 49
18 34, 50, 73, 90
18.2-31 50
18.3 51
18.8-16 50, 90
18.21-28 50
18.21-25 50, 51
18.21-24 50
18.23 50
18.25 51
18.26-30 90
18.32-51 50
18.33-37 50
18.38-43 90
18.44-49 90
19 24, 33, 36, 39, 42-45, 50, 60, 73, 85
19.2-7 42
19.2-5 43, 45
19.2 45
19.3 45
19.5-7 44
19.5 45
19.7 45
19.8-15 41, 42
19.8-10 44
19.8 43, 49
19.9-15 18
19.9-12 44
19.9 44
19.12-15 42
19.12-14 45
19.12 44
19.15 43, 46
20 99
20.2-4 101
21 99
23.7 111
24 30, 83, 115
24.4 83
24.5 83
24.7 83
24.9 83
25 54, 61, 62, 73, 83
25.1-3 62
25.1 62, 83
25.4-5 62
25.4 83
25.6-7 62
25.8-10 62
25.8 51, 83
25.9 83
25.11 62
25.12-15 62
25.12-13 62
25.12 51, 83
25.13 83
25.14-15 62
25.16-20 62
25.16 62
25.17 83
25.18 62
25.20 62, 83
25.21 62, 83
25.22 62
26 83, 110, 117
26.1 83
26.2 83
26.4-5 110
26.4 83
26.6-7 110
26.6 83, 110, 115
26.7 110
26.8 110, 111
26.9 83
26.11 83
27 51, 73, 110
27.1-6 51, 52, 110, 111
27.4 111
27.6 101, 111
27.7-14 51, 52
27.7 110, 111
27.8 52
27.11 51-53
28 99
32 17, 52, 73
32.1-2 52
32.3-5 53
32.5 53
32.6 53
32.8-9 52, 53
32.8 51, 52
34 17, 34, 62
34.8 63
34.9 63
34.10 63

34.11	63	40.14-18	47, 101	51.19	105, 106
34.12-22	63	41	18	51.20-21	105, 106
34.12	63	41.14	34	51.20	106
34.13	63	42–72	34	51.21	106, 109
34.15	61, 63	42–43	111	52	75
34.16-21	63	42	74	52.11	112
37	12, 17, 47,	42.5	111	53	61, 73, 74
	48, 57, 63-	43.4	111	53.2	61
	65, 73	44–49	74	53.3	61
37.3	61	44–47	74	53.5	61
37.25-26	47	45	30, 91	53.6	61
37.27	61	45.7-8	91	53.7	61
37.30-31	47	45.8	91, 92	54	112
37.30	64	49	17, 64, 65,	54.7	112
37.31	47, 49		73, 74	54.8	101, 112
37.35-36	47	49.2-5	64	54.9	112
38.15	64	49.2	64	61	99
39	58, 63, 64,	49.3-12	66	63	99
	73	49.4	65	64–70	74
39.2-4	64	49.5	64, 65	66	112, 117
39.2	63, 64	49.7-10	64	66.1-7	112
39.5-7	63	49.10	66	66.8-12	112
39.5-6	63	49.11	54, 64, 66	66.13-20	112
39.5	64	49.13	64	66.13-15	101, 112,
39.6	58, 63	49.16	64, 66		113
39.7	63	49.17-20	64	66.16-20	113
39.8	64	49.17	66	66.16-19	112
39.12	63, 64	49.18-20	66	66.16	112
39.13-14	63	49.21-22	66	66.18	113
39.13	63	49.21	64	69	107
39.14	63	49.22	66	69.10	107
40	47, 73, 101,	49.23-28	66	69.31-32	107
	109	49.23-26	66, 67	69.31	107
40.1-11	103	50	103	69.32	107
40.2-18	47	50.5	104, 105	70	47, 101
40.2-13	47	50.8-15	103-105	72	18, 25, 26,
40.2-11	101	50.9-15	104		33, 42, 88,
40.2-4	103	50.9-11	104		92, 99, 123
40.5	103	50.14	104, 106	72.1	92
40.6	103	50.16	19	72.5-11	92
40.7-9	101-103	50.23	104, 106	72.5	92
40.7-8	47	51–62	74	72.6	92
40.7	48, 101-103	51	75, 105,	72.8-11	92
40.8-9	103		109, 117	72.18-19	92
40.8	48, 101, 102	51.12	106	72.20	21, 86, 92,
40.9	47-49, 102	51.18-19	105		119
40.10	48, 103	51.18	103, 105,	73–89	34
40.12-18	101		106	73–83	74

73 12, 23, 24, 33, 35, 36, 63-65, 73, 74, 85, 120, 122
73.1-12 23
73.13-17 23
73.13 110
73.14 64
73.18-28 23
73.22 54
73.23-26 24
78 48, 73, 74, 99
78.1-3 48
78.1 48, 49
78.2-4 45
78.2 48
78.4-7 49
78.5-8 49
78.5-7 49
78.5 49
78.9 49
78.10-11 49
78.10 49
78.37 49
78.56 49
78.72 48
84–88 76
84–85 76
84 74, 76
84.3 76
84.5 76
84.6 76
84.8 76
84.11 76
84.12 76
85 76
85.7-8 76
85.9 76
85.10 76
86 34, 53, 73, 74, 76
86.2 76
86.4 76
86.5 76
86.8-10 54
86.11 51, 53, 76
86.12-13 54
86.12 76
87–88 76
87 76
88–89 82
88 76, 82
88.2 76
89 18, 25, 26, 82, 88, 92, 99
89.2-19 93
89.2 65
89.4-5 93
89.5 94
89.19 93
89.20-52 93
89.20-38 93
89.22 94
89.29 94
89.30 94
89.31 49
89.39-52 93
89.39 93
89.47-52 93
89.47 94
90–92 19, 81, 82
90-150 88
90-106 22, 35
90 35, 67, 68, 73, 74, 82
90.1 82
90.3-12 67
90.3-10 59
90.5-6 68
90.11-17 68
90.12 67
90.16 82
91 12, 82
91.1 82
91.9 82
91.14-16 53
92–99 77
92 54, 55, 73, 74, 77, 82
92.2 82
92.4 55
92.5 55, 82
92.6-10 55
92.6-8 77
92.6 54
92.7-8 54
92.7 54, 55, 66
92.9 82
92.11 55
92.12 55
92.13-15 54, 55
92.13 54
92.14 55
92.15 54
92.16 55
93–100 82
93–99 75, 77, 94
93 25, 35, 61, 77, 82
93.2 82
93.4 82
94 55, 73, 75, 77
94.1-11 55, 56
94.1-7 55
94.7 55
94.8-15 55, 56
94.8-11 55, 56, 77
94.8 54, 55
94.9 55
94.10 55
94.11 55, 59
94.12-23 55, 56
94.12-15 55, 77
94.12-13 56
94.12 49, 56
94.12.13 55
94.16-23 55
95–99 25, 35, 61
95 77
98 75, 77
99 77
101–106 82
102 35
104.35 19
105–107 77
105 19, 56, 57, 73, 74, 78
105.45 49
106 18, 19, 77, 78

107 56, 73, 74, 78, 113
107 (LXX) 77
107.1-32 57
107.1 112
107.8-9 57
107.8 113
107.15-16 57
107.15 113
107.21-22 57, 113
107.22 106, 113
107.31-32 57
107.31 113
107.33-43 57
107.43 56, 57, 78
110 26, 94, 95
110.1 95, 97
110.2 95
110.3 95, 112
110.4 95
110.5-6 96
110.5 95, 97
110.6 95
110.10 97, 98
110.11-12 97
110.11 97
110.13-16 97
110.17-18 97, 98
110.17 97, 98
110.18 98
111–113 35
111 19, 57, 68, 69, 73, 74, 78
111.2 57, 58, 69
111.3 69
111.4 69
111.5 58, 69
111.8 69
111.10 58
112 12, 17, 19, 68, 69, 73, 74, 78
112.1 68, 69
112.2 68
112.3 69
112.4 68, 69
112.6 69
112.8 69
112.10 68, 69
115–117 35
116.13 114
116.14 114
116.17 106, 114
116.18 114
118 115, 117
118.1 112
118.8-9 59
118.26-27 101
118.27 110, 115, 116
119 12, 18, 24, 33, 36, 39, 41, 42, 47, 49, 54-56, 60, 69, 73, 74, 85, 121
119.6 55
119.102 51
119.105 44
119.108 112
119.130 44
119.15 55
119.155 58
119.171 48
119.18 55
119.33 51
119.34 56
119.35 58
119.45 58
119.94 58
119.99 55
120–134 35
126 70
127 69, 70, 73, 74
128 12, 17, 70
130 71
131 70, 71, 73, 74
131.1 70, 71
131.2 70
132 96
132.1-7 96
132.8-10 96
138-145 35
139 71, 73, 74
139.1-18 71, 72
139.1-6 72
139.7-12 72
139.8-11 72
139.13-16 72
139.17-18 72
139.19-24 71
139.23 71
139.24 72
141 108
141.2 108, 109
144 58, 59, 73, 74, 99
144.1-2 58
144.3-4 58, 59
144.3 58
144.4 58
144.9-10 58
144.11 58
144.12-15 58
146-150 35, 81, 84, 122
146-149 19
146 59, 73, 74
146.3-4 59
146.4 59
146.5 59
146.9 19
150 18, 19, 24, 25, 32, 81, 85, 122

Proverbs
1–9 45, 52, 63, 71, 84
1.6 48, 64
1.7 58
1.8 48
1.15 52
1.23 48
2.8 64
2.13 52
2.20 52
3.1 48
3.7 70
3.23 52
4.1 63

4.2 48
4.4 51
4.5 48
4.11 51
4.20 48, 64
5.1 48, 64
5.7 48
5.13 48, 64
6.6-8 52
6.20 48
6.23 44
7.2 48
7.24 48
8.8 48
8.34 67
9.10 58
10.5 61
11.28 54
12.1 54
13.25 71
14.11 54
14.34 61
15.2 45, 48
15.11 72
15.24 61
15.28 48
15.33 70
16.17 64
16.18 70
16.19 70
16.20 61
16.23 52
17.2 61
17.3 72
17.27 61
18.12 70
19.14 61
20.24 72
20.27 72
21.1 72
21.12 61
22.4 70
23.9 45
26.5 70
26.12 70
26.16 70
28.11 70
29.23 70
30.2 54
30.15 71
30.16 71
30.24-31 52
31.10-31 84

Ecclesiastes
3.12 61
7.20 61
9.11 61

Song of Songs
6.10 44

Isaiah
1.11-17 103
1.11 100, 103
1.16-17 103
66.1-4 100

Jeremiah
3.16-17 98
6.19 103
6.20 100, 103
23.15 98
33.15 98

Ezekiel
19.11 115
29.21 98

Daniel
6.11 108

Hosea
6.6 100, 103
14.5 112
14.10 57

Amos
5.21-24 103
5.22 100, 103
5.24 103
5.25 100
9.2-3 72

Micah
5.1 98
6.6-8 100, 103
6.7 103
6.8 103

Zechariah
3.8 98
6.12 98

Malachi
1.10 105, 116

Ecclesiasticus
24.3 36
24.23 36

2 Maccabees
2.7-8 98

NEW TESTAMENT

Matthew
22.24 95
26.64 95

Mark
12.36 95

Luke
20.42-43 95

Acts
2.34-35 95

Ephesians
1.20 95

Colossians
3.1 95

Hebrews
1.8-9 91

Hebrews (cont.)
1.13 95
5.6 95
6.20 95
7.17-21 95

Mishnah
Suk.
3.8 115
3.12 115
4.4 115
4.5 115

Josephus
Ant.
3.10.4 115

INDEX OF AUTHORS

Albertz, R. 100
Allen, L.C. 108, 115
Alter, R. 23
Anderson G.W. 37, 48, 52, 55, 58, 63, 66, 67, 71, 79, 80, 92, 94, 102, 107, 115
Auffret, P. 29, 79

Barnes, W.E. 67, 70, 94, 105, 113
Barth, C. 121
Begrich, J. 107
Bennett, R.A. 61
Beyerlin, W. 57, 113
Briggs, C.A. 43, 49, 50, 52, 58, 67, 70, 71, 89, 92, 97, 104, 105, 112
Brueggemann, W. 22, 24, 27, 31, 47, 85, 122

Carroll, R.P. 48
Childs, B.S. 18, 19, 21, 28, 31
Craigie, P.C. 40, 45, 47, 50-52, 61, 63, 101, 102, 104
Crenshaw, J.L. 37
Culley, R.C. 121

Dahood, M. 40, 42, 44, 48, 57, 58, 65, 67, 69, 71, 105, 108
Dalglish, E.R. 105
Duhm, B. 43, 53, 58, 61, 67, 70, 92, 93, 107, 108

Engnell, I. 18

Gunkel, H. 12, 15-17, 23, 27, 36, 37, 43, 49-52, 55, 57-59, 65, 67, 69-71, 93, 105, 107, 108, 114

Haran, M. 108
Howard, D.M., Jr 28, 33, 82, 93

Jacquet, L. 11, 38, 40, 44, 48-50, 52, 55, 67
Jansen, H.L. 16
Jastrow, M. 67

Koole, J.L. 71
Kraus, H.-J. 40, 43, 48-53, 55, 57, 59, 66, 67, 70, 89, 92, 94-96, 102-104, 107, 108, 111, 114, 115
Kruse, H. 97, 98
Kuntz, J.K. 37

Lang, D. 17
Lescow, T. 83
Lindars, B. 40
Lipiński, E. 79

Marx, A. 108
Mays, J.L. 23, 24, 26, 27, 31, 37, 79, 81
McCann, J.C., Jr 23-26, 28, 37, 88, 93, 120
Meer, W. van der 95, 96
Meysing, J. 115, 116
Millard, M. 29, 30, 35, 119, 124
Miller, P.D., Jr 28, 32, 70, 79, 89
Mowinckel, S. 12, 15-17, 27, 33, 37, 52, 93, 102, 111
Murphy, R.E. 17, 26-28, 33, 37, 52, 79, 81, 119

Nielsen, E. 67

O'Brien, J.M. 113

Petuchowski, J.J. 115
Ploeg, J.P.M. van der 94
Prothero, R.E. 70

Rad, G. von 16, 37, 45, 67, 68
Reindl, J. 19, 21, 37, 81, 82
Reventlow, H. Graf 116
Ridderbos, N.H. 47, 101
Ruppert, L. 62

Schmidt, H. 40, 43, 50, 51, 55, 58, 61, 70, 71, 93, 101, 103, 108
Smith, M.S. 25
Steck, O.H. 44, 45, 60

Tournay, R.J. 65

Vesco, J.-L. 50, 90

Wagner, N.E. 111
Wagner, S. 72
Weiser, A. 43, 50, 52, 55, 58, 69, 70, 72, 94, 96, 101, 104, 108
Westermann, C. 18, 21, 31, 85, 120
Whybray, R.N. 15
Willis, J.T. 79, 81
Wilson, G.H. 20-22, 24, 27, 28, 31-33, 38, 85, 88, 120, 123
Würthwein, E. 71, 72

Zimmerli, W. 121

JOURNAL FOR THE STUDY OF THE OLD TESTAMENT SUPPLEMENT SERIES

28 G.I. Emmerson, *Hosea: An Israelite Prophet in Judean Perspective*
29 G.J. Brooke, *Exegesis at Qumran: 4QFlorilegium in its Jewish Context*
30 D.J.A. Clines, *The Esther Scroll: The Story of the Story*
31 W.B. Barrick & J.R. Spencer (eds.), *In the Shelter of Elyon: Essays on Ancient Palestinian Life and Literature in Honor of G.W. Ahlström*
32 T. Polk, *The Prophetic Persona: Jeremiah and the Language of the Self*
33 J.G. McConville, *Law and Theology in Deuteronomy*
34 J. Maier, *The Temple Scroll: An Introduction, Translation and Commentary*
35 G.W. Coats (ed.), *Saga, Legend, Tale, Novella, Fable: Narrative Forms in Old Testament Literature*
36 M.D. Goulder, *The Song of Fourteen Songs*
37 J.T. Butler, E.W. Conrad & B.C. Ollenburger (eds.), *Understanding the Word: Essays in Honor of Bernhard W. Anderson*
38 T.H. McAlpine, *Sleep, Divine and Human, in the Old Testament*
39 D. Jobling, *The Sense of Biblical Narrative: Structural Analyses in the Hebrew Bible, II*
40 E.R. Follis (ed.), *Directions in Biblical Hebrew Poetry*
41 B.C. Ollenburger, *Zion, the City of the Great King: A Theological Symbol of the Jerusalem Cult*
42 J.D. Martin & P.R. Davies (eds.), *A Word in Season: Essays in Honour of William McKane*
43 G.C. Heider, *The Cult of Molek: A Reassessment*
44 S.J.L. Croft, *The Identity of the Individual in the Psalms*
45 A.R. Diamond, *The Confessions of Jeremiah in Context: Scenes of Prophetic Drama*
46 B.G. Webb, *The Book of Judges: An Integrated Reading*
47 S. Soderlund, *The Greek Text of Jeremiah: A Revised Hypothesis*
48 W. Claassen (ed.), *Text and Context: Old Testament and Semitic Studies for F.C. Fensham*
49 J.D. Fowler, *Theophoric Personal Names in Ancient Hebrew: A Comparative Study*
50 M. Noth, *The Chronicler's History* (trans. H.G.M. Williamson with an Introduction)
51 P. Joyce, *Divine Initiative and Human Response in Ezekiel*
52 C.C. Broyles, *The Conflict of Faith and Experience in the Psalms: A Form-Critical and Theological Study*
53 R.N. Whybray, *The Making of the Pentateuch: A Methodological Study*
54 J. Unterman, *From Repentance to Redemption: Jeremiah's Thought in Transition*
55 T.L. Thompson, *The Origin Tradition of Ancient Israel: 1. The Literary Formation of Genesis and Exodus 1–23*

56 N. Kiuchi, *The Purification Offering in the Priestly Literature: Its Meaning and Function*
57 G.W. Coats, *Moses: Heroic Man, Man of God*
58 K.G. Hoglund, E.F. Huwiler, J.T. Glass & R.W. Lee (eds.), *The Listening Heart: Essays in Wisdom and the Psalms in Honor of Roland E. Murphy, O. Carm.*
59 B. Uffenheimer & H.G. Reventlow (eds.), *Creative Biblical Exegesis: Christian and Jewish Hermeneutics through the Centuries*
60 L.J. Archer, *Her Price is beyond Rubies: The Jewish Woman in Graeco-Roman Palestine*
61 D.G. Johnson, *From Chaos to Restoration: An Integrative Reading of Isaiah 24–27*
62 P.G. Kirkpatrick, *The Old Testament and Folklore Study*
63 D.G. Schley, *Shiloh: A Biblical City in Tradition and History*
64 C.A. Evans, *To See and Not Perceive: Isaiah 6.9-10 in Early Jewish and Christian Interpretation*
65 K. Nielsen, *There is Hope for a Tree: The Tree as Metaphor in Isaiah*
66 J. Hughes, *Secrets of the Times: Myth and History in Biblical Chronology*
67 L. Eslinger & G. Taylor (eds.), *Ascribe to the Lord: Biblical and Other Studies in Memory of Peter C. Craigie*
68 L.R. Klein, *The Triumph of Irony in the Book of Judges*
69 P.R. House, *Zephaniah, A Prophetic Drama*
70 S. Bar-Efrat, *Narrative Art in the Bible*
71 M.V. Fox, *Qohelet and his Contradictions*
72 D.N. Fewell, *Circle of Sovereignty: A Story of Stories in Daniel 1–6*
73 J.W. Flanagan, *David's Social Drama: A Hologram of Israel's Early Iron Age*
74 W. van der Meer & J.C. de Moor (eds.), *The Structural Analysis of Biblical and Canaanite Poetry*
75 R.C. Bailey, *David in Love and War: The Pursuit of Power in 2 Samuel 10–12*
76 M.Z. Brettler, *God is King: Understanding an Israelite Metaphor*
77 J.R. Bartlett, *Edom and the Edomites*
78 E.F. Davies, *Swallowing the Scroll: Textuality and the Dynamics of Discourse in Ezekiel's Prophecy*
79 P.M. Arnold, S.J., *Gibeah: The Search for a Biblical City*
80 G.H. Jones, *The Nathan Narratives*
81 M. Bal (ed.), *Anti-Covenant: Counter-Reading Women's Lives in the Hebrew Bible*
82 D. Patrick & A. Scult, *Rhetoric and Biblical Interpretation*
83 D.T. Tsumura, *The Earth and the Waters in Genesis 1 and 2: A Linguistic Investigation*
84 L. Eslinger, *Into the Hands of the Living God*
85 A.J. Hauser & R. Gregory, *From Carmel to Horeb: Elijah in Crisis*

86 A. Niccacci, *The Syntax of the Verb in Classical Hebrew Prose* (trans. W.G.E. Watson)
87 D.J.A. Clines, S.E. Fowl & S.E. Porter (eds.), *The Bible in Three Dimensions: Essays in Celebration of Forty Years of Biblical Studies in the University of Sheffield*
88 R.K. Duke, *The Persuasive Appeal of the Chronicler: A Rhetorical Analysis*
89 R. Rendtorff, *The Problem of the Process of Transmission in the Pentateuch* (trans. J.J. Scullion)
90 M.F. Rooker, *Biblical Hebrew in Transition: The Language of the Book of Ezekiel*
91 F.H. Gorman Jr, *The Ideology of Ritual: Space, Time and Status in the Priestly Theology*
92 Y.T. Radday & A. Brenner (eds.), *On Humour and the Comic in the Hebrew Bible*
93 W.T. Koopmans, *Joshua 24 as Poetic Narrative*
94 D.J.A. Clines, *What Does Eve Do to Help? And Other Readerly Questions to the Old Testament*
95 R.D. Moore, *God Saves: Lessons from the Elisha Stories*
96 L.A. Turner, *Announcements of Plot in Genesis*
97 P.R. House, *The Unity of the Twelve*
98 K.L. Younger Jr, *Ancient Conquest Accounts: A Study in Ancient Near Eastern and Biblical History Writing*
99 R.N. Whybray, *Wealth and Poverty in the Book of Proverbs*
100 P.R. Davies & R.T. White (eds.), *A Tribute to Geza Vermes: Essays on Jewish and Christian Literature and History*
101 P.R. Ackroyd, *The Chronicler in his Age*
102 M. Goulder, *The Prayers of David (Psalms 51–72): Studies in the Psalter, II*
103 B.G. Wood, *The Sociology of Pottery in Ancient Palestine: The Ceramic Industry and the Diffusion of Ceramic Style in the Bronze and Iron Ages*
104 P.R. Raabe, *Psalm Structures: A Study of Psalms with Refrains*
105 P. Bovati, *Re-Establishing Justice: Legal Terms, Concepts and Procedures in the Hebrew Bible* (trans. M.J. Smith)
106 P.P. Jenson, *Graded Holiness: A Key to the Priestly Conception of the World*
107 C. van Houten, *The Alien in Israelite Law*
108 P.M. McNutt, *The Forging of Israel: Iron Technology, Symbolism and Tradition in Ancient Society*
109 D. Jamieson-Drake, *Scribes and Schools in Monarchic Judah: A Socio-Archaeological Approach*
110 N.P. Lemche, *The Canaanites and Their Land: The Tradition of the Canaanites*
111 J.G. Taylor, *Yahweh and the Sun: The Biblical and Archaeological Evidence for Sun Worship in Ancient Israel*
112 L.G. Perdue, *Wisdom in Revolt: Metaphorical Theology in the Book of Job*
113 R. Westbrook, *Property and the Family in Biblical Law*

114 D. Cohn-Sherbok (ed.), *A Traditional Quest: Essays in Honour of Louis Jacobs*
115 V. Hurowitz, *I Have Built You an Exalted House: Temple Building in the Bible in Light of Mesopotamian and Northwest Semitic Writings*
116 D.M. Gunn (ed.), *Narrative and Novella in Samuel: Studies by Hugo Gressmann and Other Scholars, 1906–1923* (trans. D.E. Orton)
117 P.R. Davies (ed.), *Second Temple Studies: 1. Persian Period*
118 R.J. Tournay, *Seeing and Hearing God with the Psalms: The Prophetic Liturgy of the Second Temple in Jerusalem* (trans. J.E. Crowley)
119 D.J.A. Clines & T.C. Eskenazi (eds.), *Telling Queen Michal's Story: An Experiment in Comparative Interpretation*
120 R.H. Lowery, *The Reforming Kings: Cult and Society in First Temple Judah*
121 D.V. Edelman, *King Saul in the Historiography of Judah*
122 L. Alexander (ed.), *Images of Empire*
123 E. Bloch-Smith, *Judahite Burial Practices and Beliefs about the Dead*
124 B. Halpern & D.W. Hobson (eds.), *Law and Ideology in Monarchic Israel*
125 G.A. Anderson & S.M. Olyan (eds.), *Priesthood and Cult in Ancient Israel*
126 J.W. Rogerson, *W.M.L. de Wette, Founder of Modern Biblical Criticism: An Intellectual Biography*
127 D.V. Edelman (ed.), *The Fabric of History: Text, Artifact and Israel's Past*
128 T.P. McCreesh, *Biblical Sound and Sense: Poetic Sound Patterns in Proverbs 10–29*
129 Z. Stefanovic, *The Aramaic of Daniel in the Light of Old Aramaic*
130 M. Butterworth, *Structure and the Book of Zechariah*
131 L. Holden, *Forms of Deformity*
132 M.D. Carroll R., *Contexts for Amos: Prophetic Poetics in Latin American Perspective*
133 R. Syrén, *The Forsaken Firstborn: A Study of a Recurrent Motif in the Patriarchal Narratives*
134 G. Mitchell, *Together in the Land: A Reading of the Book of Joshua*
135 G.F. Davies, *Israel in Egypt: Reading Exodus 1–2*
136 P. Morris & D. Sawyer (eds.), *A Walk in the Garden: Biblical, Iconographical and Literary Images of Eden*
137 H.G. Reventlow & Y. Hoffman (eds.), *Justice and Righteousness: Biblical Themes and their Influence*
138 R.P. Carroll (ed.), *Text as Pretext: Essays in Honour of Robert Davidson*
139 J.W. Watts, *Psalm and Story: Inset Hymns in Hebrew Narrative*
140 W. Houston, *Purity and Monotheism: Clean and Unclean Animals in Biblical Law*
141 G.C. Chirichigno, *Debt-Slavery in Israel and the Ancient Near East*
142 F.H. Cryer, *Divination in Ancient Israel and its Near Eastern Environment: A Socio-Historical Investigation*
143 D.J.A. Clines & J.C. Exum (eds.), *The New Literary Criticism and the Hebrew Bible*

144 P.R. Davies & D.J.A. Clines (eds.), *Language, Imagery and Structure in the Prophetic Writings*

145 C.S. Shaw, *The Speeches of Micah: A Rhetorical-Historical Analysis*

146 G.W. Ahlström, *The History of Ancient Palestine from the Palaeolithic Period to Alexander's Conquest* (ed. D. Edelman, with a contribution by G.O. Rollefson)

147 T.W. Cartledge, *Vows in the Hebrew Bible and the Ancient Near East*

148 P.R. Davies, *In Search of 'Ancient Israel'*

149 E. Ulrich, J.W. Wright, R.P. Carroll & P.R. Davies (eds.), *Priests, Prophets and Scribes: Essays on the Formation and Heritage of Second Temple Judaism in Honour of Joseph Blenkinsopp*

150 J.E. Tollington, *Tradition and Innovation in Haggai and Zechariah 1–8*

151 J.P. Weinberg, *The Citizen-Temple Community*

152 A.G. Auld (ed.), *Understanding Poets and Prophets: Essays in Honour of George Wishart Anderson*

153 D.K. Berry, *The Psalms and their Readers: Interpretive Strategies for Psalm 18*

154 M. Brettler & M. Fishbane (eds.), *Minḥah le-Naḥum: Biblical and Other Studies Presented to Nahum M. Sarna in Honour of his 70th Birthday*

155 J.A. Fager, *Land Tenure and the Biblical Jubilee: Uncovering Hebrew Ethics through the Sociology of Knowledge*

156 J.W. Kleinig, *The Lord's Song: The Basis, Function and Significance of Choral Music in Chronicles*

157 G.R. Clark, *The Word Ḥesed in the Hebrew Bible*

158 M. Douglas, *In the Wilderness: The Doctrine of Defilement in the Book of Numbers*

159 J.C. McCann, *The Shape and Shaping of the Psalter*

160 W. Riley, *King and Cultus in Chronicles: Worship and the Reinterpretation of History*

161 G.W. Coats, *The Moses Tradition*

162 H.A. McKay & D.J.A. Clines (eds.), *Of Prophet's Visions and the Wisdom of Sages: Essays in Honour of R. Norman Whybray on his Seventieth Birthday*

163 J.C. Exum, *Fragmented Women: Feminist (Sub)versions of Biblical Narratives*

164 L. Eslinger, *House of God or House of David: The Rhetoric of 2 Samuel 7*

165 E. Nodet, *A Search for the Origins of Israel: From Joshua to the Mishnah*

166 D.R.G. Beattie & M.J. McNamara (eds.), *The Aramaic Bible: Targums in their Historical Context*

167 R.F. Person, *Second Zechariah and the Deuteronomic School*

168 R.N. Whybray, *The Composition of the Book of Proverbs*

169 B. Dicou, *Edom, Israel's Brother and Antagonist: The Role of Edom in Biblical Prophecy and Story*

170 W.G.E. Watson, *Traditional Techniques in Classical Hebrew Verse*

171 H.G. Reventlow, Y. Hoffman & B. Uffenheimer (eds.), *Politics and Theopolitics in the Bible and Postbiblical Literature*

172 V. Fritz, *An Introduction to Biblical Archaeology*

173 M.P. Graham, W.P. Brown & J.K. Kuan (eds.), *History and Interpretation: Essays in Honour of John H. Hayes*

174 J.M. Sprinkle, *'The Book of the Covenant': A Literary Approach*

175 T.C. Eskenazi & K.H. Richards (eds.), *Second Temple Studies: 2. Temple and Community in the Persian Period*

176 G. Brin, *Studies in Biblical Law: From the Hebrew Bible to the Dead Sea Scrolls*

177 D.A. Dawson, *Text-Linguistics and Biblical Hebrew*

178 M.R. Hauge, *Between Sheol and Temple: Motif Structure and Function in the I-Psalms*

179 J.G. McConville & J.G. Millar, *Time and Place in Deuteronomy*

180 R. Schultz, *The Search for Quotation: Verbal Parallels in the Prophets*

181 B.M. Levinson (ed.), *Theory and Method in Biblical and Cuneiform Law: Revision, Interpolation and Development*

182 S.L. McKenzie & M.P. Graham (eds.), *The History of Israel's Traditions: The Heritage of Martin Noth*

183 J. Day (ed.), *Lectures on the Religion of The Semites (Second and Third Series) by William Robertson Smith*

184 J.C. Reeves & J. Kampen (eds.), *Pursuing the Text: Studies in Honour of Ben Zion Wacholder on the Occasion of his Seventieth Birthday*

185 S.D. Kunin, *The Logic of Incest: A Structuralist Analysis of Hebrew Mythology*

186 L. Day, *Three Faces of a Queen: Characterization in the Books of Esther*

187 C.V. Dorothy, *The Books of Esther: Structure, Genre and Textual Integrity*

188 R.H. O'Connell, *Concentricity and Continuity: The Literary Structure of Isaiah*

189 W. Johnstone (ed.), *William Robertson Smith: Essays in Reassessment*

190 S.W. Holloway & L.K. Handy (eds.), *The Pitcher is Broken: Memorial Essays for Gösta W. Ahlström*

191 M. Sæbø, *On the Way to Canon: Creative Tradition History in the Old Testament*

192 H.G. Reventlow & W. Farmer (eds.), *Biblical Studies and the Shifting of Paradigms, 1850–1914*

193 B. Schramm, *The Opponents of Third Isaiah: Reconstructing the Cultic History of the Restoration*

194 E.K. Holt, *Prophesying the Past: The Use of Israel's History in the Book of Hosea*

195 J. Davies, G. Harvey & W.G.E. Watson (eds.), *Words Remembered, Texts Renewed: Essays in Honour of John F.A. Sawyer*

196 J.S. Kaminsky, *Corporate Responsibility in the Hebrew Bible*

197 W.M. Schniedewind, *The Word of God in Transition: From Prophet to Exegete in the Second Temple Period*

198 T.J. Meadowcroft, *Aramaic Daniel and Greek Daniel: A Literary Comparison*

199 J.H. Eaton, *Psalms of the Way and the Kingdom: A Conference with the Commentators*

200 M.D. Carroll R., D.J.A. Clines & P.R. Davies (eds.), *The Bible in Human Society: Essays in Honour of John Rogerson*

201 J.W. Rogerson, *The Bible and Criticism in Victorian Britain: Profiles of F.D. Maurice and William Robertson Smith*

202 N. Stahl, *Law and Liminality in the Bible*

203 J.M. Munro, *Spikenard and Saffron: The Imagery of the Song of Songs*

204 P.R. Davies, *Whose Bible Is It Anyway?*

205 D.J.A. Clines, *Interested Parties: The Ideology of Writers and Readers of the Hebrew Bible*

206 M. Müller, *The First Bible of the Church: A Plea for the Septuagint*

207 J.W. Rogerson, M. Davies & M.D. Carroll R. (eds.), *The Bible in Ethics: The Second Sheffield Colloquium*

208 B.J. Stratton, *Out of Eden: Reading, Rhetoric, and Ideology in Genesis 2-3*

209 P. Dutcher-Walls, *Narrative Art, Political Rhetoric: The Case of Athaliah and Joash*

210 J. Berlinerblau, *The Vow and the 'Popular Religious Groups' of Ancient Israel: A Philological and Sociological Inquiry*

211 B.E. Kelly, *Retribution and Eschatology in Chronicles*

212 Y. Sherwood, *The Prostitute and the Prophet: Hosea's Marriage in Literary-Theoretical Perspective*

213 Y.A. Hoffman, *A Blemished Perfection: The Book of Job in Context*

214 R.F. Melugin & M.A. Sweeney (eds.), *New Visions of Isaiah*

215 J.C. Exum, *Still Amid the Alien Corn? Feminist and Cultural Studies in the Biblical Field*

216 J.E. McKinlay, *Gendering Wisdom the Host: Biblical Invitations to Eat and Drink*

217 J.F.D. Creach, *The Choice of Yahweh as Refuge and the Editing of the Hebrew Psalter*

218 G. Glazov, *The Bridling of the Tongue and the Opening of the Mouth in Biblical Prophecy*

219 G. Morris, *Prophecy, Poetry and Hosea*

220 R.F. Person, Jr, *In Conversation with Jonah: Conversation Analysis, Literary Criticism, and the Book of Jonah*

221 G. Keys, *The Wages of Sin: A Reappraisal of the 'Succession Narrative'*

222 R.N. Whybray, *Reading the Psalms as a Book*